WHY WORK SUCKS AND HOW TO FIX IT

Cali Ressler and Jody Thompson are the founders of CultureRx, a company that promotes their belief that there is a better way to work. They met at Best Buy, where they first created the Results-Only Work Environment. They live with their husbands and children in the Twin Cities.

WHY WORK SUCKS
AND HOW TO FIX IT

The Results-Only Revolution

Cali Ressler and **Jody Thompson**

PORTFOLIO/PENGUIN

PORTFOLIO / PENGUIN

Published by the Penguin Group

Penguin Group (USA) Inc., 375 Hudson Street, New York, New York 10014, U.S.A.
Penguin Group (Canada), 90 Eglinton Avenue East, Suite 700, Toronto, Ontario,
Canada M4P 2Y3 (a division of Pearson Penguin Canada Inc.)
Penguin Books Ltd, 80 Strand, London WC2R 0RL, England
Penguin Ireland, 25 St Stephen's Green, Dublin 2, Ireland
(a division of Penguin Books Ltd)
Penguin Group (Australia), 250 Camberwell Road, Camberwell, Victoria 3124, Australia
(a division of Pearson Australia Group Pty Ltd)
Penguin Books India Pvt Ltd, 11 Community Centre, Panchsheel Park,
New Delhi – 110 017, India
Penguin Group (NZ), 67 Apollo Drive, Rosedale, North Shore 0632, New Zealand
(a division of Pearson New Zealand Ltd)
Penguin Books (South Africa) (Pty) Ltd, 24 Sturdee Avenue, Rosebank,
Johannesburg 2196, South Africa

Penguin Books Ltd, Registered Offices: 80 Strand, London WC2R 0RL, England

First published in the United States of America by Portfolio, a member of
Penguin Group (USA) Inc. 2008
This paperback edition with two additional chapters published 2011

1   3   5   7   9   10   8   6   4   2

THE LIBRARY OF CONGRESS HAS CATALOGED THE HARDCOVER EDITION AS FOLLOWS:
Ressler, Cali.
Why work sucks and how to fix it / Cali Ressler and Jody Thompson.
p. cm.
Includes index.
ISBN 978-1-59184-203-3 (hc.)
ISBN 978-1-59184-292-7 (pbk.)
1. Job satisfaction.   2. Quality of work life.   3. Personnel management.
I. Thompson, Jody.   II. Title.
HF5549.5J63R38   2008
658.3'14—dc22   2008001597

Printed in the United States of America

To people who work,
and know there's a better way to do it.

Success, particularly in business, comes when you can believe in people—not just those with fancy titles, but every single person with unique perspective, passion, talent, and knowledge. That's what's beautiful about what Cali and Jody have done. I love that it wasn't a top-down initiative but the results of their insight into what was best for the business.

I've always been convinced that the best ideas come from those who are closest to the customer, the customer in this case being our own employees. What Cali and Jody did was remarkable because they gave the people at Best Buy not what they *thought* they needed to succeed at their jobs but what they *really* needed to succeed at their jobs—even if it took the organization in a direction no one could have imagined.

The second thing that impresses me about ROWE is where it's going. True innovation always comes with challenge and change, and, most important, tremendous opportunities to learn. At its heart ROWE is a chance for *everyone* to learn a better way to work. There is nothing fancy about this idea, and there is no reason why it can't work everywhere. The approach lets people do what they're good at instead of what you think they should be good at. It encourages people to *contribute* rather than just show up and grind out their days.

As more people embrace this idea, more will have to concede that work is a human endeavor. Instead of shying away from that fact, embrace it. Celebrate it. Instead of insulating your organization from ideas like ROWE, tap into that humanity. Tap into that opportunity to learn.

The trend for successful companies is making them more human, not less human. It wasn't that long ago that Best Buy was a regional electronics chain. We are now a global company with 140,000 employees. What has allowed this to happen has less to do with what we sell than how we've created a distinctly human culture that lets people have fun while working hard, that lets them be themselves, that trusts them to do their jobs. ROWE fits in perfectly with those ideals.

We have also embraced this new way of working at Best Buy because it's good for business. Engaged employees are more productive, more innovative, more committed. It all gets back to that idea of unleashing the natural strengths and talents of your people. I'm eager to see where ROWE goes as more business leaders wake up to the fact that you have to pay more than lip service to the happiness and the development of your employees. Our people are what matter most.

—Brad Anderson, CEO, Best Buy

CONTENTS

Foreword   vii

INTRODUCTION: We've Had Enough . . . Have You?   1

    Voices from a ROWE: Gina   9

CHAPTER ONE: Why Work Sucks   11

    Voices from a ROWE: Kara   37

CHAPTER TWO: This Thing We Call Sludge   39

    Voices from a ROWE: Phil   61

CHAPTER THREE: A Results-Only Work Environment   63

    Voices from a ROWE: Trey   83

CHAPTER FOUR: What Time Feels Like in a ROWE   87

    Voices from a ROWE: Ami   111

CHAPTER FIVE: How Work Gets Done in a ROWE   114

    Voices from a ROWE: Javier   133

CHAPTER SIX: Why Life Is Better in a ROWE   137

    Voices from a ROWE: Beth   152

CHAPTER SEVEN: What's Next for ROWE   156

    Voices from a ROWE: Charlotte   175

CHAPTER EIGHT: ROWE Update: Beyond Best Buy   178

CHAPTER NINE: Managing Using the ROWE Mind-set   194

EPILOGUE   210

Appendix I: How ROWE Are You?   215

Appendix II: Yeah, Buts   223

Acknowledgments   231

Index   235

WHY WORK SUCKS
AND HOW TO FIX IT

We've Had Enough... Have You?

This book is based on a simple idea: Our beliefs about work—forty hours, Monday through Friday, eight to five—are outdated, outmoded, out to lunch. Every day people go to work and waste their time, their company's time, and their lives in a system based on assumptions—about how work gets done and what work looks like—that don't apply in today's global, 24/7 economy.

We go to work and give everything we have and are treated like we're children who, if left unattended, will steal candy.

We go to work and watch someone who isn't very good at their job get promoted because they got in earlier and stayed later than anyone else.

We go to work and sit through overlong, overstaffed meetings to talk about the next overlong, overstaffed meeting.

We see talented, competent, productive people get penalized for having kids, for not being good at office politics, for being a little different.

We go to work in the Information Age, but the nature of the workplace hasn't fundamentally changed since the Industrial Age.

But most of all—most tragically of all—we play the game. We play the game even though we know in our heart of hearts the game doesn't make any sense.

Why do you think Sunday night is tinged with dread? That is you telling yourself that the way we work is unhealthy. That life isn't meant to be lived this way. The modern workplace makes people physically and mentally sick, undermines families, and wastes precious time and energy. Everybody knows work sucks and yet we do nothing. If the dismal nature of work weren't the norm; if our assumptions and expectations about work weren't so ingrained; if, for example, work were some kind of new disease that suddenly appeared and cost businesses billions and ruined people's lives, you can bet that we would be marshaling our collective resources to find a cure.

So why doesn't it change?

Maybe because we assume that work has to be drudgery.
     (If it were fun it would be play, right?)
Maybe because we have been brought up to believe that
     by definition work is unproductive, political, and
     unfair.
Maybe because no one has proposed a reasonable, effec-
     tive alternative.

Everywhere there are solutions that are not solutions.

The solution is not flextime. Flextime is a joke.

The solution is not work-life balance. Under the current system, balance is impossible.

The answer is not getting better organized, or No-Meeting

Wednesdays, or setting your alarm fifteen minutes early to beat the morning rush, or spending a Saturday making all your lunches for the month.

There are no tips or tricks or helpful hints that are going to solve this problem.

There are no answers in the employee handbook.

The only solution is to change the game entirely.

We're starting a movement that will reshape the way many things in this country, and across the world, get done. We're offering not a new way of working, but a new way of living. This new way of living is based on the radical idea that you are an adult. It's based on the radical idea that even though you owe your company your best work, you do not owe them your time or your life. This new way of living is practical and simple (though not necessarily easy), and while it's a sweeping change from how we live life now, it requires only a basic adjustment in your thinking.

We are talking about a Results-Only Work Environment or ROWE^SM.

In a Results-Only Work Environment, people can do whatever they want, whenever they want, as long as the work gets done. Many companies say their people can telecommute or work a flexible schedule. But these arrangements often still include core hours, or can be dissolved should business needs change, or are doled out stingily as a perk for the privileged few. In a ROWE, you can literally *do* whatever you want whenever you want as long as your work is getting done. You have complete control over your life as long as your work gets done.

You can go grocery shopping at ten in the morning on Tuesday. You can take a nap at two in the afternoon on Wednesday.

You can go to a movie at one in the afternoon on Thursday. And you don't have to ask anyone's permission or tell anyone where you're going. You just do it. As long as your work gets done—as long as you get *results*—then your life is your own.

You get paid for a chunk of work, not for a chunk of time.

We realize that this sounds too good to be true. This kind of freedom and control and trust sounds like the stuff of rainbows and unicorns. But this idea didn't come out of the blue. The seeds of a Results-Only Work Environment started in 2001, when a leader at Best Buy corporate headquarters was looking for help in making the company an Employer of Choice. The Employer of Choice committee was an internal task force whose goal was to figure out how to make Best Buy a top consideration among talented people looking for employment. The group conducted a survey asking employees what they most wanted from work. The overwhelming response was, Just trust me with my time. Trust me to do my job and I will deliver results and be a happier employee to boot.

Enter Cali Ressler. Even though Cali was only twenty-four years old and an hourly employee, one of the leaders of the Employer of Choice committee asked her to help turn this insight into action.

This turned out to be the perfect opportunity for Cali, given where she was in her life. Best Buy was one of her first jobs out of college, and she was quickly learning the absurdities of the workplace. The veterans around the office were teaching her how to play the game, how to fill out time cards to reflect the number of expected hours (not actual time worked), how to look busy when the boss was walking the floor, how to appear "engaged" by asking lots of questions in meetings. Mostly she was learning how unhappy everyone was at work, not so much with the tasks they had to accomplish but with the whole culture of the workplace. Even the salaried employees—the people who seemed to have power and control—were always looking over their shoulder.

In an effort to respond to this misery, Cali helped create the Alternative Work Program, a pilot program that gave people a choice from a predetermined set of flexible schedules. The choices were all based on typical flextime arrangements (telecommuting; four ten-hour days; eight-hour days that started and ended at unorthodox times), but the AWP was different in two key ways. First, *everyone* in the 320-person department who took part in the pilot got to participate. The flexibility wasn't just available to top performers or those above a certain job level. Second, the employees (not the managers) decided which of the four options was best for them, and once they made their choice it was nonnegotiable. It was up to the department as a whole to figure out how to make everyone's individual choice work.

It was this control over schedule that planted the seed for what would become a Results-Only Work Environment. Cali saw that if you gave people even a little control over their time they immediately began to see the benefits both at work and at home. The people in AWP were happier and more productive and they didn't want the pilot to end.

Jody came on board in 2003, and the insights and ideas gained during AWP started to grow and change. As we developed and refined what a Results-Only Work Environment was and how it worked, the culture of Best Buy started to change. Some managers were supportive and others weren't. Regardless, the idea grew and grew and eventually took on a life of its own. By the time this book is published, approximately three thousand Best Buy corporate employees will work in a ROWE, with plans to test ROWE in the retail environment.

Thanks to ROWE, people at Best Buy are happier with their lives and their work. The company has benefited too, with increases in productivity averaging 35 percent and sharp decreases in voluntary turnover rates, as much as 90 percent in some divisions.

This book is about bringing this commonsense, effective, and mutually beneficial approach to living and working to the rest of the world. In the coming pages we'll explore why the workplace is broken and reveal the hidden attitudes and beliefs behind the problem. Then we'll describe what a Results-Only Work Environment is and how it works, and how it addresses the problem of work. You'll also get a taste of what life is like in a ROWE (hint: it is very, very good).

Along the way we won't be afraid to acknowledge the challenges a ROWE creates for an organization. The good news is that we're not advocating that companies radically change their values, their identity, or their core business. People and companies don't have to change who they are, just how they work.

In the coming pages we hope to build a compelling case for why everyone should be in a Results-Only Work Environment. We'll tell stories and give results, but we won't bully you with statistics. We doubt there is a single perfect fact out there—every year stress costs American businesses $300 billion; the average worker only puts in three hours of real work per day—that will somehow wake people up. All you have to do is Google the words *work* and *family* or *stress* and *productivity* and you'll have all the statistics you'll ever need. Presenting a rational argument for why work sucks isn't going to change anything, because our attitudes about work aren't based on reason. We need a new approach to the problem.

Ultimately what we are offering is a proven cure:

for the problem of work,
for being treated like a child by your company,
for feeling stressed-out about time.

We know it sounds too good to be true, but it's not. You still have to do your job. But in a Results-Only Work Environment everyone gets to act like an adult and gets treated like an adult.

You get your dignity back.

You get your time back.

You get your life back.

And if all that can be true, if you can have your time and work and live and be a person, then the question you're faced with every day isn't, Do I really have to go to work today? but, How can I contribute?

How do I contribute to this thing called life? What can I do today to benefit my family, my company, myself?

Changing how we work is not going to be easy. There will be a lot of resistance, and that resistance will come from surprising places (including inside you). But we need this change. As you read these words we are out there fighting to make work productive, fair, and humane for everyone. We hope that in our lifetime this commonsense approach to work isn't the exception, but the new norm.

Voices from a ROWE: Gina

Gina* works on a team that focuses on strengths-based training. She is also part of the company's diversity group. She has been at Best Buy for four and a half years and in a Results-Only Work Environment for three and a half years. She is in her mid-thirties.

I look at my parents' generation when you went to work for one company and you fully expected to be there your whole life. And then my mom got laid off and it was such a blow. Her attitude was, How could you do this to me?

My relationship with my company is different. We trade work for money. It's not personal. And I think we've come to this point where ROWE can be successful because enough people are ready to not look at employers as parents. I don't expect Best Buy to take care of me for the rest of my life. They have to treat you fairly. But in a free market, if it isn't working out for either party, then it's over.

---

*Stories like this one that appear throughout the book have been edited for clarity but are otherwise in the person's own words. The names and some of the business details have been changed to protect privacy.

I think for some managers there is the expectation that they are still kind of the parent. Becoming a manager means you're in charge. Part of being in charge means having control. That means having control over people. Often that means enforcing the rules just because they're the rules.

I have a friend at another company who was having trouble managing an employee who is a free spirit. My friend struggled with the guy because he wasn't around as much, but he was his best employee. My friend said he wanted to give him higher-level work but he couldn't because being in the office for a certain number of hours was part of what they measured people on, and this employee was failing.

To me this is financially irresponsible for that organization. Why did anyone care how long that guy was there? What kind of message does that send? If I build a cot under my desk but I'm not performing, does that make me a good worker?

I have another friend who is an economist and a college professor, so he's already living in a Results-Only Work Environment. It's just not called that. Still, his idea of what work should look like is based on this old corporate model. He once said to me, "They must need you at your desk. Otherwise they wouldn't have given you one."

So I like to talk to him about how being measured by results is a much better measure than time at your desk. I try to put it in economic terms. From the employer's point of view, the risk that someone is not at their desk is worth the reward. The risk is that they will not do their job. But you can't monitor someone 24/7, so that risk is there anyway. But the reward of giving them freedom is if they actually do their job they will stay at their job longer. Once you've been in a ROWE and have that power, you don't want to work anywhere else.

CHAPTER ONE

Why Work Sucks

I've been late to work for the last three days, and I'm starting to get "the eye" from my boss. This morning, I race to get ready and get into my car with an hour to make a commute that usually takes me about thirty minutes. Plenty of time to get to the office by eight, and maybe even by seven forty-five to get a few extra points. Then I see it. Traffic backed up two stoplights behind the entrance ramp to the freeway. No way. There's construction on the other route I could take, so this is my only bet. I start sweating and panicking, knowing this will knock me back at least an hour, putting me at the office at nine, not my wishful seven forty-five. I'm positive I will be fired, or at least put on a warning for being late four days in a row. I can feel my blood pressure rising, my heart racing, and I so badly just want to step on the gas and fly down the shoulder as far as I can go. I reach for my phone, knowing what I have to do. I fight with myself because what I'm about to do feels awful. I convince myself that if I don't do it, I will lose my job. I dial my boss's number. I get his voice mail. I cough and say, in a raspy voice, "Jim, I'm just not feeling well today. I don't think I'll be able to make it in. I was up all night with a fever. [Cough, clearing throat.] I'll see you to-morrow."

I'm so excited—my husband and I have plans to go to dinner at my favorite restaurant to celebrate our anniversary. The restaurant is an hour away and to make our six o'clock reservation during rush hour, I'll need to leave work at four thirty. Leaving at this time is unheard of where I work, but tonight I don't care what anyone says about me. I arrive at the office and find out that my boss has called a surprise meeting with my team. She proceeds to tell us that she hasn't seen the dedication she needs to see on our new project. She expects to see us all working until at least six every night to "put in our time." I talk with her after the meeting to let her know that I'll be leaving at four thirty for my anniversary dinner, but I'll work until seven every other night this week. She glares at me and lets me know that there are people lined up for my job—I can make my own decisions. I know, in that moment, that my husband and I will need to celebrate this weekend instead of to-night. I cancel our reservation and call my husband. He asks me when I'm going to realize what's really important in life and hangs up the phone. I ask myself the same question as I lay my head down on my desk.

Why does work suck?

If you ask people why work sucks they will usually give one of two answers. They will reach for something vague—it's a hectic world; people are busy; that's life. Or they will latch onto something specific to their workplace—a controlling boss who clocks every minute of every break, an unfocused management team that creates a constant state of emergency.

But we would argue that the answer is both deeper and more widespread. There are systemic problems that every workplace shares. The details change from person to person and place to place, but the underlying problem is the same. And it's a bigger problem than life being hard or that business now travels at blinding speeds.

Work sucks in corporate life today because we have time all wrong.

Just look at the two stories above. The first person wants to "score points" for coming in fifteen minutes early. The manager in the second story expects people to stay until six because that somehow shows dedication. Coming in late four days a week might cost you your job. Staying late every night might get you that promotion. You can't leave at four thirty and you better not come in at nine. And at no point is there any discussion of the quality of the work being done. It's just time, time, time.

We all labor under a myth:

Time + physical presence = results.

When it comes to work our attitudes about time are so omnipresent they are almost invisible, and here are two trivial examples that we have picked exactly because they are so offhand and random. When New York mayor Michael Bloomberg gave the commencement address at the College of Staten Island, he said some good things to the future workers of America about taking risks and learning how to collaborate with people, but he put the most passion and force into this statement:

"If you're the first one in in the morning and the last one to leave at night and you take fewer vacation days and never take a sick day, you will do better than the people that don't do that. It is very simple."

We think that's a strange sentiment coming from the mayor of New York. We're not knocking having a solid work ethic, but when we think of the individuals who have made it in the greatest city in the world, we think of their creativity, innovation, savvy, and competitiveness. We think of people who have brought something to the table—whether it's in art or finance or government—that no one else has brought before. We certainly don't think about people putting in hours.

The other example typifies the kind of career advice we give people who work in nontraditional work environments. It's from a website that offers tips to freelancers for how to be successful:

"Log your time and work. As you have no time clock and no one to watch over you, you need to account for your time, if not for your employer or your client, then for yourself. It's important that you not have a day go by without knowing what you've really accomplished, so log what you do, and how long it takes. It may seem like extra work, but really it just takes a few seconds after every task."

This is interesting, as if you wouldn't know the quality of the work you've done if you didn't also judge it in terms of time. The line "if not for your employer or your client, then for yourself" says it all. The assumption is that you need to keep track of your time for more than billing purposes. Without knowing how long a piece of work takes you can't measure its true value.

This unwritten rule about time applies to just about everybody, from administrative assistants on up to the senior leadership. With the exception of sales people, who either deliver their numbers or don't, most people are judged by a mixture of results and time spent in the office. You are expected to do your job and to complete your tasks, but you are also expected to put in forty hours or even more.

Strangely we only do this at work. If you're out running errands on Saturday and getting things done, you're not measuring yourself by the clock. You might be frustrated that a specific chore is taking so long, but you don't look at a pile of laundry and think, I'd better make sure I'm putting enough hours into this. You either accomplish what you set out to accomplish or you don't. If anything there is incentive to get things done more quickly and efficiently because then you'll have more time to do something else. At work, even if we accomplish our tasks we are expected to fill the hours. Because by definition a full-time job takes forty hours or more to complete.

Why do we look at time in this way? Maybe it's a relic of the Industrial Age, when if you weren't at your place on the assembly line then the work wasn't getting done. If you didn't put in your time the job didn't get done. Or maybe this attitude about time goes back even further, back to when most people worked by hand. If you were practicing a craft, then time put into making a cabinet or a suit of armor would have more directly translated into a quality piece.

There was a time when the forty-hour workweek served a good purpose. We owe the forty-hour workweek to the Fair Labour Standards Act of 1938, which also ended the practice of child labour and established the minimum wage. The idea was to make labor uniform and fair back when companies had too much control over workers' lives. But somehow the forty-hour workweek morphed into the gold standard for competency, efficiency, and effectiveness.

In an information and service economy it doesn't make

sense to use time as a measurement for a job well-done. What does forty hours even mean? And what does forty hours get you? Naturally it still takes time to do research or build a body of knowledge or build relationships, but the individual actions we take every day, the little units of work have more to do with communication and problem solving. Today we do more work with our brains than with our hands, and knowledge work requires a different set of assumptions about productivity.

Knowledge work requires fluidity (ideas can happen anytime, not just between eight and five) and concentration (being rested and engaged is more important than being on the clock) and creativity (again, you're either on or you're not on, regardless of the hour). Today we spend our lives performing in jobs in which it's harder to measure effectiveness in terms of time. After all, how long does it take to think of the answer to a colleague's question? Or to have an insight about the marketplace? Or to say the right thing to close a sale?

When we try to live our lives under this new set of demands but under the old set of assumptions, we get the stories that opened this chapter. We get burned-out, frustrated people struggling to reconcile the old and the new. So what? you might say. These kinds of anecdotes are so commonplace they almost don't seem worth mentioning. That's life, right? Everyone has moments like these at work. There is something about time that stresses everyone out. If the workplace is unfair it's unfair for everyone. Don't call it the end of the world. Call it Tuesday.

We agree that these kinds of stories are ordinary and even mundane, but we doubt that you could find anyone who would argue that they are evidence of a workplace that is ideal. And we bet you could find a lot of people who might wonder how much longer we can go on like this. At this level of stress. In this toxic atmosphere. At this relentless pace toward a goal that no one can see because no one has defined it. We've gotten used to the working world, but does anybody like it? Is anyone truly benefiting? Few individuals are giving their best. Few companies are getting the best from their people. The fact that we get time wrong in corporate America may seem small, but those small moments add up to big problems both for employee and business.

One of the most recognizable consequences of our misplaced faith in time is Presenteeism. Let's take Bob, for example. Bob has mastered the politics of corporate America. Now in his late fifties he has seen it all—downsizing, outsourcing, rightsizing. But he has continued to rise through the ranks because he knows how to play the game. He gets in before everyone else, scoring that sweet parking spot by the front door, the one where everyone who comes in later can note with a mixture of envy and resentment that Bob outdid them again. During the day Bob goes to every meeting. He eats lunch at his desk. He turns the lights out at night. His bosses describe him as "a workhorse" and "a rock." You can't deny that he's working, right? He puts in so much time. He must be doing something!

No matter that Bob doesn't really *do* anything. No matter that Bob hasn't contributed meaningfully to the bottom line in years.

At some time in our lives, most of us, whether we like to admit it or not, are guilty of Presenteeism, which is any time you're physically present and putting in time, but you're not really doing your job. Your body is in the building, but your mind is somewhere else.

Presenteeism is when you're at your computer playing

World of Warcraft or shopping on eBay or keeping tabs on the NCAA tournament. Presenteeism is when you're on time for work but then spend an hour online reading the paper. Presenteeism is when you're constantly telling people that you're there for them, that you're available, that you have time for their concerns, but you're not doing everything you can to solve the problem at hand, often because you're not exactly sure what the problem at hand even is. Presenteeism creates a mentality that leads to statements like this:

"I finished that project a day ahead of time, but don't tell anyone. I don't want to hand it in early or else the boss will just dump more work on my desk."

"Team, we're giving Jan the Employee of the Month award today. She put in some really long hours last month, and I have a feeling she was even here on the weekends. We're lucky to have such a dedicated, committed player on our team. Let's give it up for Jan!"

"Paul, I've seen you leaving before three pretty often lately. You know, as long as you're putting in your forty hours, it doesn't bother me if you leave early. There have been some complaints from the team, though. Some folks have seen you putting in twenty-five to thirty hours in the office. Let's step that up. As you know, we have a lot of work to do."

But this mentality begs some important questions:

If you are getting your job done, then why are you punished by having to fill your time?

If you are adding value to the company, if you are performing, then who cares if it takes you forty hours or forty seconds to do it?

If you are skating by, filling the hours, watching the clock, then what are you doing with your life?

We're not calling out individual employees. In fact, just the opposite. Presenteeism doesn't happen because people are lazy or unfocused or not dedicated to their work. Presenteeism happens everywhere, every day, because the way we measure work performance is wrong. It's a flaw in the system, not in the people.

Our false worship of time distorts behavior. Because we're not just doing our job but making sure our job fits into a forty-hour workweek that happens between eight and five (with a half hour or an hour for lunch) we have to jump through hoops to make the job fit the clock.

The clock turns us into liars. We call in sick when we have to take care of family business. Or we put in long hours to make up for not being able to accomplish the task at hand.

The clock disrupts engagement. On any given day you either feel overworked (I can't believe I have to do all of this in forty hours!) or underworked (I can't believe I have to be here for forty hours!).

The clock discourages innovation and creativity. You can't be motivated to solve the company's problems because even if you do you are still judged on how much time you put in. You can't serve two masters.

We aren't blaming this all on The Man. Our attitudes about time are so ingrained that we are all guilty of this kind of misguided thinking. Even those who work for a progressive company—even those who are in a largely results-driven work culture—aren't immune from these outdated attitudes.

> We show up at work and instead of thinking about what
> we can do to drive results, we try to figure out
> how we can both accomplish our goals and do it in

a way that fits within the narrow confines of an eight-to-five day.

We feel admiration (or envy) for the people who log the most hours at work because we feel they are somehow working harder.

We complain about how many hours we're putting in, as if this makes us heroes.

We eat sometime between eleven thirty and one thirty and only for an hour, because that is the acceptable time to eat and the acceptable duration for eating.

We're skeptical that people who are on flextime programs are putting in enough hours to do their job.

We worry that coming in at eight fifteen will brand us as being "late." Or we get excited about coming in at seven forty-five so we can be seen as being "early."

We don't question for a minute that work should be measured in terms of time, that some jobs are "part-time" and others are "full-time" and that forty hours is the norm.

When we talk to people about these attitudes we find that people understand that the system is broken. When we first started creating the model for what would become a Results-Only Work Environment, we didn't need to tell people that attitudes about time were misguided. Everyone knew it intuitively, and once we started giving them the opportunity to talk about these unwritten rules it was like a revelation.

Before the Alternative Work Program was formalized at Best Buy, Cali was charged with running focus groups for the 320 people who were going to take part in the experiment. A typical group was made up of 10 to 15 people and they were a mixed bag of hourly employees, lower-level salaried employees, and upper-level management. The goal of these groups was to figure out how to create a program that addressed this somewhat amorphous issue of trust. A lot of the comments were all over the map and addressed technical concerns (making sure there was good communication, clear goals, feedback tools to monitor how the pilot was going), but the refrain was that people were desperate to get control over their time.

There was an epic sadness to these meetings, because everyone knew what they were missing. Even if they didn't articulate it this clearly, they knew that their jobs were robbing them of precious time. Time with their friends and family. Time for professional development. In some cases—if they were triple booked for meetings all day long—even time to do their jobs.

Why do we put up with this? Where does time get its awesome power over our lives? You might think that some important researcher and thinker has done a long-term, multivariable study that proves that we need to have this business model based on time because the data shows that people who aren't working at least forty hours can't be effective in a global, 24/7 economy. But you would be wrong. We have these attitudes about time and we let time have this power over us because of one thing:

Belief.

The advice from Mayor Bloomberg and the freelance success website is not only an illustration of how misguided we are about how we think about time, but also an example of how flimsy our thinking is when it comes to work in general. We're not bashing them. Instead we'd rather show that the foundation of our assumptions about work has gotten shakier and shakier as technology and globalization have changed the world.

Look at Addie. Just out of college, she is new to the workforce. Addie is a smart and capable employee. She grew up one of those kids whom people label "overscheduled" but while her life is very full, she's also excellent at managing her priorities. In college she was the type of student who got good grades, had a boyfriend, took part in extracurricular activities, and was able to make it all work. She's an effective, dedicated worker, but while her career is important to her, so are her friends and outside interests. For her, all aspects of her life matter.

Unfortunately her attitude about life isn't sitting well with her manager and the rest of her team. She likes to work at odd hours and at coffee shops, but her boss says that that doesn't fly. According to her manager, the other people on Addie's team don't like it when she leaves the building to get some quiet time to work, or when she asks to leave early on Fridays, even though she's completed her work. On one hand, Addie draws praise from her boss, who notes that people like her and appreciate her contributions. "You have great ideas," Addie's boss says. "But if you're coming and going all the time you won't get promoted. People won't take you seriously. After all, perception is reality."

Perception is reality.

How many times have you heard that expression with regard to work? Maybe you've said it yourself or something like it.

"Better look busy. I hear the CEO is on the floor today."
"It's not what you know but who you know."

"I have to make that meeting. It's my only chance this
        week to get face time with my boss."

The funny thing about these attitudes about work is that
they aren't taught in school. You don't learn about how the
workplace works in a class. There are books about how to get
ahead in business or how to make friends and influence people,
but there aren't books that teach you how to behave at work.
There is no resource for normal.

So where do these beliefs come from? We learn about work
from watching our parents and elders experience work, from
the stories they tell. We hear advice like Mayor Bloomberg's
or get some coaching from our mom or dad about how to act
professional before going off to our first job. But mostly we
learn about what is normal at work by experiencing it. One of
the lessons work teaches us right away—whether we're working at a restaurant or doing grunt work in an office or mowing
lawns for our neighbors—is that there is the job you do and
the job you appear to be doing.

You have your tasks and responsibilities, aka The Job.

You also have the sometimes unwritten and unspoken rules
that you have to play by, aka Work.

These unspoken and unwritten rules are based on beliefs
that we all share about how work gets done and what it looks
like to get work done. We have so many beliefs about work it
would be impossible to name them all. Here is a partial list:

- Most work happens from Monday to Friday, eight to
  five.
- People at their workstations are doing work.
- Results are proportional to efforts.

- "Summer Hours" programs help create work-life balance for our employees.
- People who work a lot of hours get more work done than people who work fewer hours.
- Nonexempt employee status is a way for us to protect our employees from working too many hours.
- Working "out of hours" is not good for work-life balance.
- Flexibility creates performance issues.
- People in flexible work environments don't have enough time to get their work done.
- If people can get their work done in less time, they should get more work.
- The best customer service happens face-to-face.
- Creating more "jobs" helps us manage more work.
- Face time is necessary in order for work to get done.
- Instant availability is the measure of great customer service.
- Roles and responsibilities bring clarity to work.
- Job descriptions help people know what's expected of them at work.
- Restructuring requires longer working hours.
- If you give people control over their schedules, they will take advantage of the system.
- Managers with direct reports cannot work from home.
- The best collaboration is done face-to-face.

In an information- or service-based economy, do these orthodoxies make sense? Or are they relics of a time when we worked in a certain way because there was no alternative? Before technology, we *had* to go to the office because that's where we kept the mimeograph machine, the landline, the Liquid Paper. We invented "management by walking around" because you couldn't leave someone a voice mail or create an internal website to monitor the progress of a project. People couldn't work virtually because there was no virtual, only physical space and real time.

We have all these assumptions about what work looks like even though in today's economy work looks less and less like it did twenty years ago.

Dig, if you will, these pictures: one of a woman walking her dog, another of a man sitting in a conference room with some other men.

Now ask yourself: Which one of them is working?

If it was fifty years ago you would automatically assume that the man was working. For one, most women didn't work. For another, what kind of work could she possibly be doing while walking the dog? Also, just look at that man! He's right there! In a conference room in an office building, a place where work gets done! True, he is just sitting there and we can't know his thoughts, or if he's even paying attention, or if he's had a worthwhile idea in recent memory. Who knows? Maybe after this meeting he's about to be fired. But he looks like he's working.

In fact, even today, with women in the workplace, we're still likely to make all kinds of assumptions about these two people, that work happens in certain kinds of places, at certain times, with certain kinds of people. Beliefs about work have been formed over generations and now they're so ingrained that people don't even question them. And yet, read almost any business success story and we promise you that the inspiration for that new product, service, or company didn't happen in a cubicle. The stories of great brands like Starbucks or great companies like Apple start out in the world, or in an inventor's garage, not in a conference room with eight people staring at a flip chart.

But still we cling to these old ideas even though we're stifling ourselves. Just look at poor Addie. She's bright and capable. She blazed through college juggling all aspects of her life. So why does her boss assume that the only way Addie can get her work done is if she is in her cube from eight to five? What is this weird thing about how Addie won't be taken seriously if she doesn't put on a show of work (as opposed to simply doing her job)? Why do we accept nonsense like "perception is reality"?

In fact, our assumptions about how work gets done and what work looks like are so entrenched that any alternative, even an effective one, is treated as comedy. Take this opening to a Reuters article from July 18, 2000, titled "This Friday, Make It Real Casual."

"This Friday is the first National Work at Home Day, an occasion when there won't be any need to feel guilty about negotiating a multimillion-dollar deal in your boxers and bunny slippers, or interviewing a chief executive while wearing just a towel."

Isn't that interesting? Why would someone who just negotiated a multimillion-dollar deal have to feel guilty about anything?

Our beliefs about where and how work gets done distort how we evaluate work just as the power of time does. Certainly work can get done in a cubicle or in a meeting, but does it have to get done that way? If one of your business contacts is calling you on the phone with a question, do they really care if you are in your cube or at the gym? We have very little "face time" with our overseas partners and yet doesn't our work still get accomplished with them? Most of what we do is trade information and ideas (and often electronically). There isn't the absolute need for us to congregate in offices.

But what about meetings? What about teams? We'll spend more time on meetings and management in the coming chapters, but for now we'll just say this:

Everyone knows that for every productive meeting there are at least two more that aren't.

Everyone knows that once a meeting reaches a certain size it's likely that at least three people will be there who don't have to be there.

Everyone knows that a good portion of what is accomplished in a meeting—meaning the actual exchange of information—could be handled through e-mail.

We think the point of meetings is to get work done. But meetings are also a way of expressing and exercising our outdated beliefs about work. This is why people who are double and triple booked are seen as more important than people who don't have as many meetings. This is why people who can make other people go to meetings are seen as powerful, even if this power has nothing to do with effectiveness. This is why you can skate by in a job just by attending lots of meetings, because if you showed up then naturally you contributed. The work that gets done in meetings is fine. The unwritten and unspoken rules that surround meetings are one of the big reasons why work sucks.

As Gina noted in her story, there is a definite risk-reward

equation at work if you don't give people control over their time and their work. If you let your beliefs about work serve as your guide, you are robbing yourself and your coworkers and employees of the control they might even need to do their jobs. Just when you need to be as fluid as possible, just when you need to be lean and mean and thoughtful and wise and nimble and proactive and all those business things you need to be, you are hamstrung by assumptions. You're stuck in a cube with a desktop computer and a phone with a cord so you can be there in person should your manager walk over to check up on whether or not you're working. The game becomes looking busy instead of working hard and solving problems and contributing. It's a game no one wins. You lose your freedom, your motivation, your soul, and in exchange for control over your life, your company often gets little more than a show of work.

None of this is written down anywhere. Employee manuals have time and vacation policy guidelines, but people don't walk around living by the rule books. The culture at a workplace is a living, breathing thing. So how do these beliefs get reinforced?

Let's take Heather as an example. Heather might be the unhappiest person at her company. She's in her early forties, recently divorced with two kids who are in day care. She is the only person making that family go. She's not always the best worker, but she's better than most and she can really pour it on when it counts. Her problem is that her life is killing her. No matter how hard she works there is always something that isn't getting done. Personal life or work life—neither is flourishing. She puts her kids in day care when they are sick and feels bad all day. She's constantly being taken to task for her attendance. Her coworkers treat her like a fallen woman. Sometimes the cues are subtle—like when the room goes quiet when she walks in—but other times people say it to her face, that if she can't seem to manage both family and work then maybe she should find another job. Over time this all adds up, until it gets to the point at which even the slightest comment can deflate her. One day she is fifteen minutes late for a morning meeting that hasn't really started yet. As she enters the room her boss looks up and says, "Nice of you to join us," and as sad as it sounds, this little jab pretty much destroys her whole day.

Human beings judge everything—especially other people. Their attire, their hair, their driving, their cooking, their speech, their financial well-being, their occupation, even their child-rearing skills. We make judgments automatically, and sometimes we choose to say out loud what's in our heads. Some people are outwardly cruel, cutting down their friends and family with barely veiled references to their shortcomings. Some people are well-meaning but unthinking, making otherwise innocent comments about how much money someone makes, how their marriage is going, their weight, their hair.

Still there are rules. Part of growing up is learning what you can and cannot say to people, what is polite and what is rude. Strangely, at work a lot of these rules don't apply. We have this weird permission to be shitty to one another at work. We judge people's perceived work habits. We judge how we imagine people's personal lives and personal choices affect their work. We especially judge people about how they use their time.

We say:

"Coming in at eleven again? Boy, I wish I had your
    hours!"
"Another vacation—how many vacation days do you get?
    I haven't taken a vacation in five years!"
"How in the world could John get a promotion? He's
    never even here!"
"I wish I smoked. Then I could always be on break and
    never have to work."

We call this kind of judgment Sludge[SM]. Sludge is the negative commentary that occurs naturally in a workplace and is based on outdated beliefs about time and work.

We'll go into Sludge in more detail in the next chapter, but for now let's just say that Sludge performs a very important function at work. When we judge people—when we Sludge them—we are expressing outdated attitudes about time and about what work looks like and how it gets done. We judge to make a point that someone else is different. We judge to make the point that even if someone's crime is small, they are acting outside the rules of work. We judge to make ourselves look better, to show other people (and ourselves) that we're the hardest working, we're the most dedicated. Most of all we judge them to *reinforce* those unspoken beliefs about work. It's a vicious cycle.

Time is the misguided measure.
Beliefs about work give time more power than it deserves.

> Acting on their beliefs, people judge (or Sludge) one another
> to give time power and reinforce the status quo.

When you look at work through this lens, then even seemingly "innocent" phrases start to take on deeper meanings.

"Ten o'clock and just getting in?"

The person who says this believes that work can only take place from eight to five in a physical place. They're telling you that you better start coming in on time or you'll be branded as a bad worker.

"I'm not surprised Bill got that promotion. He's always here!"

The person who says this believes not only that if you're not at work you can't be doing work, but that if you aren't seen "working" then you'll never be recognized for your achievements. They're reinforcing the idea that the people who work the longest hours must be getting the most done.

"Rita is in the lactation room again. I wish I had kids. I'd never have to work."

Translation: People who have children aren't as committed to their jobs because they're seen as not available for work. They also work fewer hours, which means they can't make a positive impact. This person is sending you a warning that if you take your career seriously, having kids can be a detriment.

As you start to hear what's really behind these kinds of comments (or catch yourself making them) you'll begin to realize how sick work is. How our sense of time and our beliefs about how work gets done are really holding us back. When we judge one another in this way, we're championing a system that distracts us from what really matters (results) and focuses our energy on what doesn't (time and place). We walk around feeling guilty and incompetent (or making other people feel guilty and incompetent), either sleepwalking through the day by filling up the hours, or by having to craft elaborate work-arounds to a system that couldn't be designed any better to retard accomplishment.

Next time you're at work, try listening for Sludge. The next time people are gossiping or venting about another employee's work habits, listen to the underlying assumptions being made about that person. You will hear lots of strange beliefs about time and place. You will hear assumptions that have nothing to do with whether or not that person is actually doing their job, but rather the way they behave at work. You might also hear what is ultimately behind every piece of Sludge: the sound of people feeling out of control. In each of these judgments there is a core truth. I have no control. I have no control over this broken system, and so I'm forced to judge other people based on rules that I instinctually know are wrong.

If the game is to prove that you're putting in time at the office, then of course you're going to judge someone who isn't putting in their time. If you have no control over when and how you work, then of course you're going to feel jealous and resentful of some-one who appears to be free. If the game is unfair but you can't change it, your only choices are to suffer in silence or to vent.

If Sludge is the sound of people feeling out of control, for management it's also an excellent means of control. Think back to the story about Heather. If you're not at work at eight then you're not performing. Somehow in the space of fifteen minutes or half an hour she went from a good employee (on time at eight every day!) to a bad employee (nice of you to join us). Using nothing other than the big hand and the little hand, her boss put Heather under her thumb, and for what?

Seemingly innocent comments tell us everything about what a workplace values. We care more about time and the appearance of being dedicated and present than we do about actual performance. We care more about controlling people than about letting them succeed. We'd rather have order than excellence.

This is why you can change jobs every year and still find yourself running into the same problems with work. This is why the love you feel in the job interview eventually sours when you find out how the place really works. This is why even "progressive" companies or "young" companies can still suck. It's not the finer points of your workplace—it's every workplace. It's not the bad boss or the unfair break policy. It's the very nature of how we work.

Time, belief, and judgment are one way of looking at the problem of work, but before we move to the next chapter, we'd like to offer another. There are two opposing forces at work on your life: demand and control.

Demands push at you from one direction, and they include things like doing your job, taking care of yourself and your home, staying connected to your family and friends. These are the basic ones. People also have demands put on them from a sick or aging parent, volunteer work, a neighborhood association, a city league softball team. Even the need to sit back once in a while and read a book counts. A demand is anything you require to live your life.

The tool for pushing back against demand is control. Imagine a typical Saturday. You might run errands, have time with family and friends, go to a movie, eat lunch, pay bills, whatever. Because you're in control of your time on Saturday you have the freedom to satisfy those demands as you see fit. You might eat lunch at three thirty instead of a traditional "lunch-time" because you'd rather catch a movie at noon and eat afterward. You might get up an hour early and pay bills and shop online to get those chores out of the way before the rest of the house wakes up, and you do so without resentment because you're choosing to get through the low-value work so you can enjoy what matters to you most. But in the end it doesn't matter how you go about your day. It's your day and as long as everything gets crossed off the list, you have no one to answer to but yourself.

When people have high demands and high control, their life can be hectic but manageable. They figure out what needs to be done and when.

When people have high demands and low control, their life is both hectic and miserable. There is nothing to figure out. They are trapped in a system that piles on the demands but denies them the control to meet those demands.

This is why work sucks. You have all these demands coming at you, from real concerns like actually accomplishing the task you've been hired to do, to dealing with the daily nonsense of getting to work on time, sitting through meetings, standing around the break room pretending to celebrate a coworker's birthday, and so on. And not only do you have the demands of work, but while you're at work the demands of the rest of your life go unattended, and you have little to no control over how and when you can meet those demands. Your time is not your own, so you do the best you can and feel like crap for not doing any one thing as well as you'd like.

The challenge then is to increase your level of control so you can effectively meet demands. We're not advocating that people do less work. Not at all. If you have five projects, *you're still going to have five projects.* What we're advocating is that all of us, both employer and employee, acknowledge that people's demands are getting higher and higher, and since you can't make those demands go away, then we absolutely must give everyone more control over how they meet those demands.

If you don't give people more control over how they meet the demands of work and life, people aren't going to be able to give their best at either. If people can't give their best at either you get a world much like the one we have now, where people are both unhappy and unproductive.

Fortunately, we live in a time when this is possible. Today technology gives people incredible power over time and information. In our personal lives, technology means we don't have to wait for the store to open to buy something. We don't have to watch our favorite show the minute it airs or come down from Mount Everest to make a phone call.

And yet when it comes to work we suddenly have to give up all these choices. We can be strong and nimble and powerful in our personal lives and yet are forced to be slow and tradition bound at work. Technology *seems* to have changed the game—people telecommute and do business via BlackBerry 24/7—but we are still playing by the old Industrial Age rules, the rules of the factory floor and the typing pool.

The laptop is colliding with the punch clock.

We're not techno-evangelists. A Results-Only Work Environment isn't about the wonders of technology. Frankly, we couldn't care less about the latest gadget. But this is about what technology *could* let us do and how we're not taking full advantage.

Most people rush to work at the same time every day when it might be more effective to work at home for all or part of the day. You eat at your desk to *show* you're available, when you might be just as reachable eating your sandwich in the park down the street. You're punished for not being present, when there are plenty of times you've been present and doing a lot of nothing.

We waste a lot of time playing by these old rules at work even when our personal lives point to a better way. It's not that time and physical space don't matter anymore, but time and space certainly matter less. We have the practical tools to meet the demands in our lives. If only we could change our minds.

Unfortunately, knowing why work sucks isn't enough to change it. If you get rid of a broken culture there still needs to be something to take its place. That new culture is a Results-Only Work Environment, but we're not ready to be in a ROWE yet. First we have to change all those outdated attitudes. We have to challenge our beliefs, and we have to start getting rid of the judgment that goes with them. All that Sludge is weighing us down, but if people can't judge one another based on those outmoded beliefs about work and time, then they can't reinforce the old rules. If we can get rid of Sludge, then work doesn't have to suck.

Voices from a ROWE: Kara

Kara is a designer who supports the dot-com division. She is in her early thirties and has been with Best Buy for nine years. She's been in a ROWE for three years.

When my team first started ROWE our Sludge session was fresh in our minds, and we all made numerous jokes about it. We were testing the waters. Were we in this together or not? Was this ROWE thing real? Someone would get up to leave and they'd be teased about going to a movie and people would watch the interaction. Would the person feel guilty and sit back down? Or would they laugh and keep walking? If someone didn't return an e-mail after three hours the slacker jokes would start. Would the person get defensive? Or laugh it off and ask what was needed of them?

This went on for a while until the day when my manager put on her coat to go home after lunch, and she squelched the jokes and called us out on our Sludge. This was the end of the jokes, as we realized that she was fully on board and ROWE was real! It was a great day. If our manager does it, then so can we.

Still, in the beginning it was frustrating to know that someone was shopping while I was in over my head with a deadline; until later, when that same person was in over their head and *I* was shopping. I didn't want to be Sludged by my coworkers, so I didn't Sludge them. When my coworker told me that he spent an afternoon helping his son with his curveball, I told him how wonderful I thought that was. It was my way of letting him know that I expected the same reaction from him when I exercised my freedom. My whole team shared this mentality of support, which was very important in stopping Sludge and making a successful ROWE environment.

Later I realized that a big difference between my team (where we didn't Sludge each other) and the team in the next aisle (where everyone spent every day in the office) was our manager. She trusted us. She saw that we continued to meet our deadlines, and she also wanted a work-life balance for herself, and so she stopped the Sludge the way we were trained to.

In addition to a manager who fully supported ROWE, I had a team that really wanted ROWE to work. We were open and honest about any challenges that ROWE created. We had frequent, honest discussions in our team meetings. This kept us from turning Sludge jokes into a passive-aggressive way of communicating our frustrations.

Not having Sludge allows me to really feel like my work and life are in balance. I still have those crazy stretches of weeks where I probably put in more than forty hours, but now I have times when I get to shut off my computer at noon and do whatever I want with my time, Sludge (and guilt) free!

CHAPTER TWO

This Thing We Call Sludge

I n the last chapter we talked about the need to change the fundamental nature of work, but isn't there an easier solution? It seems that people are feeling that the current way of work is too rigid and uniform, that if the workplace loosened up a bit some of these problems surrounding time and the way work looks would go away. Then maybe people would feel more in control. Isn't the answer just giving people a little more flexibility? Can't telecommuting or flextime give people what they need?

No.

We hesitate to slam flexible work arrangements. We'd hate to see someone who's begged and pleaded and cajoled and maneuvered to have a four-day workweek feel undermined.

But flextime is nonsense.

Companies aren't stupid. They know they need to say they're flexible to attract talent. We challenge you to find a major corporation that doesn't have a flextime section of their employee handbook—a section filled with relaxed, smiling faces and promises of understanding, freedom, and control.

But when you compare your idea of flexibility to your

company's view of flexibility you'll find a big gap. Even companies with the best of intentions can't deliver on their own promises, because flextime doesn't solve the core problem of work. In fact, traditional alternative methods of work are actually part of the problem.

Let's go back to Addie, our new, young employee. Addie looks at her employee handbook and notices that her company offers a flexible work arrangement option. She's excited. If leaving a little early on Fridays after finishing her work isn't acceptable on an informal basis, then maybe she can formalize the flexibility by taking advantage of the company's policy. She realizes that if she could just telecommute on Fridays, then she could get a jump on her weekend while still meeting the needs of her team.

But her manager is cool to the idea. First she says that that program is really more for people who have a proven track record with the company. Addie counters that even though she is new she has gotten nothing but glowing reports on her work. Furthermore she says she is willing to address any performance questions as they go and if it's not working to make the appropriate changes. Addie's boss immediately agrees that whatever arrangement they might come up with would certainly be under great scrutiny. "We can't just have people off doing whatever," she says. Then her boss says that in fact it would probably be better to revisit this idea after they clear their current slate of projects. Addie pushes and says she thinks she can handle it now, that between voice mail and e-mail and secure remote access to the company's computer system that it won't even be that different from her being there. Her boss says that it's probably not best. People are already talking about her laissez-faire attitude toward time, and maybe Addie should first buckle down for a few months and show everyone that she is committed to the company by keeping regular hours. Then they can talk. "But I have to warn you," Addie's boss says. "It's a long shot. There are a lot of people in line ahead of you for a perk like this. Let's face it. If I let you do it then I have to let everyone do it."

Addie's encounter with her boss shows the three main problems with traditional flexible work arrangements. First, there is almost always limited access depending on seniority, title, or job description. Flextime or telecommuting is for managers and directors, not administrative assistants or entry-level people. Flextime or telecommuting is for people who have project-oriented work, but not for people who are part of a daily process, such as people who work in a call center or on a customer service line. Those "frontline" people have to have their asses in a seat.

Most of all you have to earn the right to be on a four-day week. Flexibility with your hours or the ability to work from home are the kind of ultimate perks for those who are so good, so accomplished that they can flout convention and strike out on their own. You have to earn these privileges, even though all you're doing is shifting from five eight-hour days to four ten-hour days, even though you're still doing the same job. Only rock stars get to have a say in how they spend their time.

Second, flexible work arrangements are conditional. They are a privilege that can be taken away at any time based on the needs of the business, not the employee. We have a copy of a pamphlet from a major computer company that touts their understanding of people's need to work more flexibly. (You know they mean it because the cover shows a picture of a pile of rocks balanced each on top of another to show, you know, balance.)

But the more closely you read the pamphlet, the more that pile of rocks starts to look precarious. Employees still need to work core hours; they might lose their flextime if there is a perceived business need; and each person's capacity to participate in the program will be assessed on an individual basis and will be subject to periodic review to make sure both employee and company needs are being met. In other words: flexible!

But the real killer is the price you have to pay for a flexible work arrangement. Because these programs are by definition special, anyone who participates in a flexible work arrangement has to worry about suspicion from their boss ("They aren't working regular hours so how do I know I'm getting a full workload out of them?" "On the days they're not here how do I know they're even working?") and envy from their coworkers.

Have you ever heard anyone in your office praise the work ethic or the accomplishments of a coworker on a flexible schedule? Aren't you more likely to hear doubts about their commitment or digs about their availability or even open resentment that they get to do whatever they want?

We're back to the idea that "perception is reality." At companies around the world people opt out of flexible work arrangements for fear of committing career suicide. Some managers will even come right out and say that working under those kinds of arrangements is not the way to advance. And even if management is supportive, your coworkers often aren't. Even when you're at a relatively progressive company or a younger company, if you're working in a nontraditional manner you still have to prove yourself just that little bit more. People feel obligated to report their progress to justify their absence. Because at any time the old norms could snap them back into their place. Who needs the hassle?

The reason for this is that even though flexible work arrangements might seem to give people control, your work is still evaluated based on the old rules of work.

And what do those rules say?

People who aren't in the office and therefore physically available all the time aren't really working.

People who work from home aren't really working because work takes place in an office.

People who work from home are taking advantage of the company by watching *Oprah* and eating cake and ice cream while lounging in a hammock and not working.

Ultimately, people who telecommute or work four-day weeks can't be trusted because they're not in the office, where they can be seen working. (Or, as we've discussed, looking like they're working.)

The issue here is trust. People just want to be trusted to do their work. They want to be trusted as adults in the workplace, adults who will do their jobs. Everyone knows what trust feels like and flexible work arrangements are not about trust.

We trust you! (But during our busy season we may ask you to come into the office on Fridays so everyone's here to do their job.)

We trust you! (But let's check back in six months to make sure this new arrangement is working out for everyone.)

We trust you! (But we don't trust Bob. Programs like this are only for director-level employees and higher.)

This is what we call the Flexibility Con Game and it makes people miserable. Because the only thing worse than complete mistrust is mistrust masquerading as trust. It's draining and demoralizing for employees to have to listen to management pretend to trust them while behaving as if they don't. Nothing makes you feel more out of control than to be given the illusion of control, while underneath it's just demands, demands, demands. As opposed to being a way to make work suck less, flexible work arrangements actually reinforce the status quo. In fact, flextime can make life suck more.

Let's go back to Addie and say that somehow she overcomes her boss's objections and the hidden rules and secret codes behind the company's flextime program. Now what is her life like? In some ways she finds that she is more aware of time and more aware of the need to show her face to make sure people know she's working. Instead of freedom and flexibility there is now an extra layer of misery to her job. She hears things like this from her team and manager:

> "We're not going to loop you into the decision-making on this project. It's too critical and since you're not here every day we can't risk not being nimble."
>
> "It's really too bad that you're not here every day. Sometimes it feels like we have to work harder to make up for your not being here."
>
> "There are some Fridays when it would be nice to be able to stop by your cube and ask you a quick question."

No one can point to any concrete failings on Addie's part. She is still doing her job and making her deliverables, and between her cell phone and e-mail she has never missed a beat.

But still there is no such thing as a clean day. She doesn't get credit for the hours she works on Fridays and even though she's getting her job done on Fridays she feels a mixture of worry and guilt that she's not in the office. She knows people are talking about her behind her back and even worse she has internalized a lot of these complaints. Even though these comments seem to be based on envy more than on any real dissatisfaction with her or the job she is doing, Addie finds herself imagining conversations in her head and preparing defenses for her behavior. She works extra hard to have lots of ideas and insights so when someone lets loose a sarcastic "Oh, you're here today!" she has a genuine idea as a comeback. The worst part about this for Addie is that it's making her question her competence. Even though all of this misery is based on attitudes about time and beliefs about how work gets done, she mistakes it for performance. There is a pall over her entire life.

She is, in short, drowning in Sludge.

The kind of flak Addie took from her boss is modeled after the problems that started to surface halfway through the Alternative Work Program. Even though AWP wasn't a true Results-Only Work Environment, the power it gave employees to choose their schedules did make a big difference. The 320 people in the pilot reported lower stress and increased engagement and higher productivity. Overall, they were happier than they ever had been at work.

Or at least until they had to interact with other people in the company who weren't in AWP. When the employees in the pilot program were with one another everything was fine. They had adapted to their new way of working. Their managers supported them. But once they stepped outside the AWP bubble all those good feelings went away, because the rest of the culture not only didn't support what they were doing, but even tried to undermine them.

> "How can you expect to support retail if you're never here?"
>
> "Oh, you're on that flextime thing. So do you get anything done?"
>
> "AWP sounds nice, but you'll never get promoted if you're not here."

Like flextime policies around the country, AWP turned out to be a giant judgment generating machine. But the difference this time is that we recognized what was happening. We could see from the very beginning that if this idea of giving people more control over their time was going to work it had to happen companywide.

By the time AWP was winding down, Jody was brought on board as the corporate change agent responsible for working with Cali to take this idea to the next level. Jody's background included work on the Strategic Alliance team, whose responsibility it was to develop partnerships with other companies. Jody's specific role was to develop processes for overcoming cultural differences between the company and its alliance partners. Jody understood the importance of culture in making real changes. If you tried to train people to behave differently without addressing the underlying culture, you were lost. The unwritten rules would trump the written rules every time.

It seems like a small thing, but as we saw in the last chapter, culture doesn't have to be in the foreground to be powerful. As we started discussing how AWP could grow into something larger we knew that Sludge was the key to everything. As long as there is Sludge, work will continue to suck. But if we can challenge our outmoded attitudes about time and how work gets done—if we can eradicate Sludge—then we can move toward a new way of working and thinking about work.

Getting rid of Sludge is not always easy, and it continues to be a goal (and sometimes a challenge) for individuals and teams as they live life in a ROWE. But getting rid of Sludge changes everything.

So what exactly is Sludge?

As we began to discuss in chapter one, we define Sludge as any negative comment we make that serves to reinforce old ideas about how work gets done. Another way of looking at Sludge is as a kind of code for the status quo. We can't come out and say what we want to say, so we talk around it.

Someone says, "Eleven o'clock and you're just getting in?" because they can't say, "That's not fair! I got in at eight like everyone else."

Someone says, "*Another* vacation? How many vacation days do you get? I haven't taken a vacation in five years!" because they can't say, "You're a slacker. Only people who sacrifice their time are committed to their jobs."

Someone says, "I can't believe Toby got that promotion. He's never here!" because they can't say, "I don't get it. I turn out the lights at this place every night, so why am I being passed over?"

One of the things that makes Sludge so dangerous is that it seems so small. So what if people make jokes once in a while about people coming in late or missing a meeting? Who cares if someone's feelings are bruised? Work isn't supposed to build self-esteem and make us feel good about ourselves, right? That's why it's called work.

Maybe, but let us offer this story. In 2003, when we started bringing ROWE to the company at large, we weren't as sophisticated in our terminology or our teaching methods. Sludge hadn't been named yet. We hadn't fully articulated our ideas about time, belief, and judgment. We were flying by the seat of our pants. We had no manual, but we knew to focus on culture.

Today a Sludge session lasts an hour and a half, and we cover all the different types of Sludge you'll read about below. When we first started, however, the sessions were only half an hour, and rather than give the meeting shape we just asked people to volunteer all the judgments people fling at one another at work. (We highly encourage you to try this with your friends.)

One group we'll never forget came up with more than a hundred bits of Sludge in twenty minutes. Someone would start a riff about working mothers and five other people would pile on the judgment. Then entry-level people. Then older workers. Then smokers. Then people who work from home. Then people who never come to meetings. It was like watching jazz musicians trade solos. And the most amazing thing about it was that afterward no one who was in that room could honestly say that these kinds of judgments in the workplace

1. are warranted,
2. contribute to the bottom line, or
3. are anything other than a pernicious distraction from the real work at hand.

This session was also a turning point for the development of a Results-Only Work Environment because we started to notice certain themes. The different kinds of Sludge fit into buckets. There were times when people seemed to get themselves ready for Sludge, which may or may not come (Sludge Anticipation). There were times when people would go through an elaborate pantomime to explain why they were five minutes late and how they were going to work extra hard that day (Sludge Justification). And there were those especially choice times when two people or a group of people would make nasty comments about a person who wasn't there (Back Sludge or a Sludge Conspiracy).

When we were first starting out we just told people to stop judging one another. We told them to put a jar in the break room—anytime someone flung Sludge they had to put a quarter in it. But now we saw that the different types of Sludge would need to be eradicated in different ways.

Before we get to eradication, however, we need to expand upon the different kinds of Sludge because they have subtle but important differences.

Sludge Anticipation is the mental preparation we all go through if we are expecting a piece of Sludge. Let's say you're a qualified, capable employee who is in no immediate danger of losing your job, and you're running fifteen minutes late for work. Do you simply not give your lateness a second thought? Or do you start running through excuses in your head for why you're late? If you're like most people—even in the most results-focused company—you're probably trying out different excuses in your head. You're anticipating the snarky comment, and maybe stressing out a bit about your boss's or your coworkers' negative reaction. Even if the Sludge you get is good-natured and gentle, it still feels like a shot.

So on one hand Sludge can be something very small—a little dig, a joke. On the other hand, Sludge is very big. Even if it hurts someone's feelings only slightly, it's still negative and it's still undesirable. Sludge Anticipation wastes time and energy, two things that in business and in life are never in enough supply.

In the example above, the qualified, hard-working person is expending energy and time for what? To justify a measly fifteen minutes? Even if it were an hour would it matter that much? As important as your job might be, most of us are not open-heart surgeons. The patient isn't going to die on the table if we come in at eight thirty versus eight.

The worst part about Sludge Anticipation is the way it reinforces those old, broken norms. Sludge Anticipation is what enables a culture of fear in which you'd rather call in sick than have to worry about getting slammed for being late, in which you're nervous about taking too long a lunch, in which you feel like a kid who's done something to piss off your parents, even though you're not quite sure what.

Every second you spend anticipating a piece of Sludge, every second you spend coming up with excuses for being late or for skipping an irrelevant meeting, you are reinforcing this culture of fear. The worst part about it is that we do this to ourselves. We've so internalized these rules and expectations that we will punish ourselves for being late even if no one says a word. And when we "waltz in" a half hour late and no one says anything what do we feel? Relief! It's like we got away with something. And what did we get away with? A little bit of time that frankly shouldn't belong to anyone but us.

So if Sludge affects us personally more than we realize, what else is it doing to our lives? Sludge Anticipation is unnecessary, but we have only begun to waste our own time, other people's time, and our company's time. Now we enter the realm of Sludge Justification.

Let's say you get to work fifteen minutes late and you get hit with that piece of Sludge. "Oh, look who's here." Then you have to justify yourself, and because of the rules of work, because you're judged based on time and what work looks like, you can't say, "Yes, I am here and I do a great job, so why do you care?" Instead you have to make up an excuse based on time. You were stuck in traffic, there was an accident, your kid wasn't feeling well, or the cable guy came over and you had to let him in or blah, blah, blah.

Who cares? During this entire exchange you and your co-worker are standing there at work not working and spending all this time having a conversation that does what? When someone says to you, "Oh, look who's here," they are wasting their time judging you, Sludging you, and you then have to waste time defending yourself. You are also likely to tell a white lie, because the reasons we are late are usually so small they don't sound important enough to justify our misbehavior.

Then there is the aftermath of the exchange, when you waste a little more time shaking it off, rolling with it, getting to your desk, and starting your job. Let's say you're not a high performer who is ultrasecure in your job. Let's say you're new or you're in a division where there are layoff rumors. Then what kind of morning do you have? If you're like most people you are going to worry about being fifteen minutes late. You might spend the rest of the day worrying about the consequences of being late, and while you're worrying you're not as focused on the task at hand. In fact, you might come in early and stay late for the next two or three days and worry a little more not only about being late, but whether or not people are going to notice you making up the time.

All this expended time and energy and at no point has anyone thought for a second about the outcomes the business was trying to drive.

All this expended time and energy to do nothing more than reinforce the status quo that doesn't work.

All this expended time and energy over a few lousy minutes.

The thing about Sludge is that it doesn't take much of it in your day to have a negative impact. Take any company that is struggling, or any division or group that is having a hard time with the actual business at hand, or one with poor leadership or intense market pressures, and a culture of Sludge can erupt like an algae bloom. And the more a company buys into those old attitudes about time and beliefs about how work gets done, the more Sludge can run rampant. It can even become an integral part of how people socialize.

We call this Back Sludge, or, if there are enough people, a Sludge Conspiracy. This is the watercooler talk that we've all witnessed or taken part in. You can hear it almost any time you get people together at work and the conversation turns away from the business at hand (or what was on TV last night) and the daggers come out for whoever is not in the room. Kara's comment about how other people would view her department getting control over its time wasn't paranoia. Every company has a person, team, or department that other people slam when they're not around.

"Those IT people are always goofing off. They should try doing a real job instead of playing around on the computer all day."

"Those smokers are practically always on break. I think
     I'll take up smoking. I might get lung cancer but at
     least I won't have to work as hard."
"Rick isn't getting any younger; he should retire and make
     room for someone who isn't a hundred years old."

Just look at these examples and think about what is behind
them. The first one says that work that involves socializing
with clients isn't real work. The second one says that the time
in your chair is more important than your ideas. The last that
old people can't possibly be effective. But each of these comments serves a larger function. In its sick, twisted way, Sludge
brings people together. This is old-fashioned tribalism. You're
in my tribe. That person over there is not. When you create a
Sludge Conspiracy you're really saying, "We play by the rules.
We're good workers. That person over there is not."

When we Sludge in groups we are also creating a public
mask for our own deficiencies. You don't have to be responsible for results as long as you clock in your time. You don't have
to be competent if you can make someone else look incompetent. You don't have to have ideas if you can make someone
else look stupid.

Every Sludge Conspiracy just reinforces these bad attitudes. You might feel temporarily superior to someone else for
bashing their work habits, but you gain nothing. If anything
you reinforce the bars of your prison. Because if you slag someone for being fifteen minutes late, you'd better believe you'll
be fifteen minutes late yourself someday. And then you go
from being the Sludger to the Sludgee.

Sludge, even in small amounts, holds us all back. We could
give the laundry list of what this kind of behavior does to

businesses—reduces engagement, lowers motivation, slows down the organization—but what it really boils down to is common sense:

When you're giving Sludge or receiving it or anticipating it you're not contributing to work or to your life.

When we allow Sludge we're accepting and reinforcing a workplace that values time and appearances over genuine accomplishment. If you were judged and paid based on what you actually contributed to your organization, then time and place wouldn't be a factor. You could be the person from the previous chapter who negotiated the multimillion-dollar deal in their boxers. But as long as there is Sludge, then you have to feel guilty about not being in the office where the "real work" gets done.

As long as there is Sludge, you'll never be free.

We have to eradicate Sludge.

Once you get wise to the existence of Sludge you start to see it everywhere. It can be a liberating feeling, like you now have a word for something that you've known about your entire life but couldn't quite name. Seeing Sludge everywhere can also make you feel gross. And it is *everywhere*. You find it in your home, at work, with your friends. You start getting attuned to all of the strange and unfair ways we judge people.

Some of this is human nature. There is a certain amount of Sludge that will never go away, and when it comes to Sludge in your family or community or in the world of politics, there may be no answer.

But work is another story, in part because there is an expectation to be professional. Even though we don't really behave the way we should, we're supposed to be neutral, objective, calm, and fair. This expectation is one of the few norms about work that is beneficial. The key is to make that norm more than lip service. And that requires the eradication of Sludge.

When people move from a traditional work environment to a ROWE we call it "migration." It starts with a team kickoff where we introduce the ideas of time, belief, and judgment. We give them a language to describe why work sucks. We introduce Sludge.

The reason for this is simple. If there is no Sludge, then it's harder (or even impossible) to reinforce the status quo. If you take away people's ability to judge themselves and others based on time, then it's harder for time to be used as a measure for performance. If you take away people's ability to judge themselves and others based on what work looks like and how work gets done, then it's harder for beliefs about work to be used as a measure for performance. Getting rid of Sludge is the first step, the crucial step, toward creating a Results-Only Work Environment.

This might seem like a big job. Sludge is pervasive, universal, and in some cases, even fun. How do you eradicate it from an entire workplace?

The first thing people need to do is refrain from giving Sludge. This is simply a matter of being more aware of the way we judge people in the workplace. Everyone is different. Some people are more obsessed with how work looks. Others are time minders. You have to search your own soul for your own contribution to the status quo. Are you a clock-watcher? Do you keep silent note of other people's hours? Or are you biased toward personality? If you're in a meeting, do you assume that the people who keep to themselves and listen aren't contributing? (Or vice versa: Sometimes we judge the overly talkative as using conversation to mask the fact that they don't have anything concrete to add.)

Once you find out what your biases are, try to look at people in another way. We're not saying that you have to be nice to everyone or that you have to be a better person. We're only asking that you act like a better person. You're going to judge people, so judge them on their performance, on their ability to meet goals. Take time and place out of the equation. (You can still judge people as incompetent, but it has to be for the right reasons.) Cutting down on your Sludge output is pretty doable. You just have to keep asking yourself, What needs to get done? Is this person (or am I) delivering or not? Everything else—when they come in, how much time they spend in their cube, how long their lunch lasts—is no longer your concern. We think you'll find just doing this to be liberating.

Remember the break room Sludge jar that some teams installed in the early days? The funny thing was that those jars remained largely empty. Once we identified Sludge and once people knew what was at stake (that if they could get rid of Sludge they would get more freedom and control over their time) no one wanted to do it. People thought, Even if it's just a quarter I don't want to do it. I don't want to be the jerk. I'd rather focus on results.

But of course we can't control other people's behavior toward us. So the next thing to get rid of is Sludge Justification. The great thing about Sludge Justification is that all those excuses that you make up, all those things you say to prove you're dedicated (I know I'm late but I'll work extra hours today to make up for it) can be knocked out with one question:

"Is there anything you need?"

The Sludger gives their Sludge: "Your kid seems to get sick a lot. Aren't you worried that it's going to interfere with your career?"

You say, in a calm, professional, and nondefensive way, "Is there anything you need?" or, "Is there something I can help you with?"

If said with sincerity, if said in the spirit of really trying to help the person (in other words, in the spirit of doing your job), you will find that this stops Sludge in its tracks because now instead of talking about misguided assumptions, you're talking about what needs to get done. The issue now is not whether or not your kids are hampering your career but what that person specifically needs from you right now.

Often you'll find that the Sludger doesn't really need anything at all. They were just flinging crap around.

But there are times when someone does need something. So you give it to them. And if they complain about your availability, bring it back to the work. "Did you try calling me or e-mailing me?" or, "The deadline for that is Friday. We're on track. But if there is something we need to discuss then let's talk about it."

The point here is to always redirect focus back to the work. The Sludger, even if they don't realize it, wants to have the conversation based on norms. They are trying to dominate or control or undermine based on time and beliefs about how work is done. The karate chop you can deliver is to bring the conversation calmly and positively back to the work. You ignore the comments about time and the need to be physically present and talk only about the work.

We realize that this isn't easy. People have said to us, "Isn't that rude to redirect the conversation like that? Isn't that disrespectful?" At first people felt guilty pushing back in this way, especially if the person doing the Sludging wanted something or needed something. People were still hung up on the idea of availability rather than performance.

The irony of this is that what's disrespectful is for the person to ask you why you weren't there at eight in the first place. Furthermore, the person who is mad at you because you weren't in your cube at eight better have a very good reason. When you say "Is there something you need?" people are exposed for their poor planning. Their poor planning was the reason they didn't get the report when they wanted it, not that you weren't in your cube at eight. (And, as we'll see in later chapters, it doesn't matter if the person doing the Sludging is your boss. In a Results-Only Work Environment, everyone's time is respected.)

You would be amazed at the effect this shift in focus has on the workplace. We'll see in future chapters how not talking about time makes the workplace much different. Emergencies don't seem like emergencies anymore. There is more planning. Problems actually get addressed instead of deflected with promises to put in more hours or stay late. You spend more time talking about the actual work, and, not surprisingly, more work gets done. The tone of the workplace also improves, because it's also really hard to judge people based on what doesn't matter when you're focusing on what does.

This focus on results—knowing that you can deflect Sludge with a well placed "Can I help you?"—makes getting rid of Sludge Anticipation easier. Because what you really should be asking yourself is not, "What kind of excuse can I come up with?" The question you really need to ask yourself—and not just when you're running late—is, "Am I doing my job?"

Because if you're performing and meeting expectations, nobody should be able to say boo.

Finally, you need to work on getting rid of Back Sludge, to avoid taking part in the Sludge Conspiracies. This can be a hard one. It would be easy to say that all you need to do is simply not participate, but we realize that we're talking about how people socialize. When people are being bitchy about coworkers it feels good to be included in the conversation. And people do say funny things about other people. It can be hard not to laugh. Furthermore, it's uncomfortable to call other people out for their Sludge, but that is what you need to do.

If someone makes a comment about time you need to redirect back to the work.

If someone says, "Jan is always taking breaks. She's never here when I need her," you can say, "I've never noticed her breaks. She's always gotten her work in to me when I needed it." Or, "Have you talked to Jan about what you need?" Or, "What do you need that Jan isn't providing? Maybe I can help you."

Now, if Jan isn't doing her job, then the idea isn't to cover for her incompetence, but the point of eradicating Sludge is to focus on the work, not the time. If Jan isn't performing, then sixty hours of work are probably not going to make the difference. Perhaps there is another problem, a training problem or miscommunication about deliverables or who knows? But as long as we're ganging up on people about time, then we will never know. If you focus on the work, not only will you eliminate Sludge but you also might even find out why Jan isn't doing her job.

Always focus on the work. This will eradicate Sludge in almost every case. If you focus on the work, then you can't attack other people, you can't gang up on your coworkers, you can't beat yourself up.

Sludge says:

You're not committed.
You're only valued based on the hours spent in the work-
    place.
You're not trusted to be left unsupervised.
You're not worth being respected.

Focusing on the work says:

Let's stop pointing fingers and solve the problem.
Let's not get caught up in office politics and instead get
    the job done.
There is no time for this bullshit. We have work to do.

No Sludge.

Voices from a ROWE: Phil

Phil is a process improvement specialist and Six Sigma black belt. He is in his early forties. He has been in a ROWE for three and a half years.

There is this misconception that ROWE is about giving people more time with the kids. A ROWE is not about having more time or having time off. You may not work fewer hours. You may even work more, but you do it on your terms.

I see a ROWE as an intense focus on business results. You focus on business results and you ignore what doesn't matter. Usually when people talk about ROWE they talk about the calendar. This is the last thing I talk about. When you finally stop talking about the calendar, you have completely entered the ROWE mindset—because you're truly focused on results.

Work culture makes people do and say things that don't drive results. The ROWE mindset is the opposite. In a ROWE, I now do what I know is right for the customer. If I'm a good employee, then I'm going to do what I know is right. It's not what company culture says is right. It's what personal culture says is right. What happens in corporate America is that people don't have the right to speak up for what they think is the best way to get the job done. They are given a job description and hours to fill, but they don't have the right to stand up for what they know their customer needs or wants. Their work culture keeps them from doing and saying the things that will drive outcomes.

I was in a meeting today and I said that if I wrote down everything I heard that we'd like to accomplish I'd have forty-six goals. My coworker said, "What's wrong with that?" We have to stop kidding ourselves. This idea that you're supposed to think big. You're supposed to be everything to everyone. You're going to be all things to the world. And then when you're forced to cut back to what's really important, it's a failure. Reality feels like a failure.

For me the beauty of a ROWE is that you remove all those elements, like the forty-six goals, that get in the way of the good job you could be doing. You take the list of what you could do this year and you focus on getting it shorter. You stop kidding yourself and you focus on the customer. All of a sudden in a ROWE all kinds of extra capacity shows up in the calendar because you're focused on the results. That's a ROWE. More and more choice and more and more control for the people you're supposed to be working for: the customer.

CHAPTER THREE

A Results-Only Work Environment

I n the early stages of developing a Results-Only Work Environment we weren't as keyed in as we are today on how a ROWE creates an intense focus on business results. In fact, during the first phase of training, when around 30 percent of Best Buy employees had migrated to a ROWE, we were still talking a lot about the calendar.

Back in 2004 we helped define a ROWE using a calendar exercise. Depending on who was running the session, Cali or Jody would put a random month on the wall and then ask people to choose when they would like to work in the building, out of the building, or not at all. The employees were then given red, green, and yellow markers and asked to put a dot on a day for when they were not working (red), when they were working out of the building (yellow), and working in the building (green). We said, "do whatever you want." Put a not-working dot on a Wednesday, put a working-in-the-building dot on a Sunday. As long as the work gets done it's up to you.

After a dozen or so people put their dots on the calendar we all stepped back and looked at the big picture. A cynic might think that the whole calendar would be filled with red dots, but that was not the case at all. Even though this was just an exercise, people didn't abuse the idea. They still put up plenty of green and yellow dots, but it was on their terms, and when we stepped back and looked at the whole month we immediately noticed two things. One, there was never a time when people weren't working. People were still going to do their jobs. For a lot of managers in the room this was a relief, and, for some, even the glimpse at an opportunity. In a 24/7 economy it could be a great benefit to be able to have people solving problems and accomplishing tasks throughout the month. Bonus.

But the employees also saw that they could be comfortable working in a nontraditional way. They might have put a red dot on a Thursday, but there were always plenty of yellow and green dots from their coworkers. They wouldn't have to feel guilty for "slacking off" on a Thursday, because there were other people contributing. They would have their time to carry the load on another day.

But the calendar exercise also raised some challenging questions that pushed at the boundaries of our beliefs about work. For example, we'd ask people if they put a red dot on a Wednesday, did they need to take a vacation day? People would hesitate and then someone would say, "No. As long as the work is getting done then it doesn't matter." Or we'd ask them if they were working at home on a Monday did they need to put an out of the office reminder on their e-mail. Again they would hesitate and then someone would say, "No. As long as I've got my cell phone and I have access to e-mail it doesn't matter where I am. I'm working and people can get ahold of me, so who cares?"

These kinds of conversations were what led us to solidify our ideas about time, belief, and judgment. The more we did the calendar exercise the more we came to understand what Phil was talking about in his story. We'd start with time, but eventually we'd be talking about the work.

In fact, as more and more people started to migrate from a traditional work environment to a ROWE, word started to spread throughout Best Buy. People would come into the training sessions with smarter questions. It started out with us pushing employees to challenge their assumptions, but then the employees started to make us challenge our own.

People started to put red, yellow, and green dots on the same day. They realized that there was never a day where you didn't think about work in some small way. They started to talk about how total control over their time couldn't be confined to days. It had to be fluid enough to work throughout the day. They wanted to get up and answer e-mails at six, then take the morning off to spend time with their kids, then come into the office in the afternoon to have a meeting, then go to a movie and then wrap things up at night. They wanted total control.

The employees didn't want the core values and identity of the company to change, but as the work culture started to change, we recognized that both our message and our methods needed to evolve.

In those early days we called ROWE a Results-*Oriented* Work Environment. The ever-changing calendar showed us that "oriented" didn't take the idea far enough. Flexible work arrangements are "oriented" toward employee empowerment but when push comes to shove it's still the old game of hierarchies, chains of command, and the military model of management. After we had been implementing ROWE at Best Buy for a year or two we realized that the only way for this idea to work was if it were a Results-*Only* Work Environment. In other words, results and *only* results are what everyone uses to measure performance in the workplace. If people were going to have total control over their time, the only measure could be results. Eventually this led us to what would become the simplest definition of a Results-Only Work Environment:

Each person is free to do whatever they want, whenever they want, as long as the work gets done.

Let's take the first part of that definition: Each person is free to do whatever they want, whenever they want. What does that mean?

The closest analogy is college. In college you know what you have to do to learn and to get good grades. You have to go to class, study the material, do well on tests or papers or in labs. And depending on the grade you want you can gauge for yourself how hard you want to work, what kind of extracurricular activities you select, how involved you want to be with your professor's research or the inner workings of the department. Depending on what you want out of college you might even be careful about the types of people you hang out with.

A college student has complete control over when and how their work gets done. There are rules of thumb, but ultimately it's up to the individual. You learn pretty quickly that boozing every night with trust fund slackers is probably not the ticket to an A. Also, no one stands over your shoulder while you're reading your textbook and says, "Study that! No, wait! Study that!" Even classes, which *seem* mandatory, are in fact optional. (It's not advisable to skip all your classes, but ultimately it's your choice.) Furthermore, you are expected to be ethical, academically honest, and fair in your dealings with faculty and other students. Whatever you want, whenever you want, doesn't mean you can lie, cheat, and steal. Even though there is freedom, there are still rules.

Probably one of the hardest things about college is that for the first time in your life you're pretty much on your own to figure out what's important to you, how you study best, where your strengths and weaknesses are as a reader, writer, and thinker. But that's also the fun of college. You choose the results, and then you drive the behaviors and attitudes that will get those results.

This is what happens in a Results-Only Work Environment. If you get results, then anything else you do with your time is completely up to you. What work looks like in terms of where it takes place and during what hours is no longer important. You work when and how you work best. You are in complete control.

Like college there are also larger expectations. You are part of a team, part of a division, part of a company. If you choose to party and play Hacky Sack in the parking lot and do D-minus work, then, rather than getting a stern word from the dean, you might get fired.

This idea of completely letting go of the way we're used to working makes a lot of people uncomfortable. As we'll see, it can be a struggle for management to let go of this kind of control over their employees. A lot of people's gut reaction to this idea is that it's too big a change. If you give people complete control over getting their work done, that means completely giving up the old model of work. This is exactly the point of a ROWE, but that's not easy for some people to take.

For example, look at the following online posting that was written as a response to a *Business Week* cover story on ROWE. The poster, writing under the name *sheezheer*, embodies this attitude that some flexibility is okay, but complete employee control would be chaos:

"We have the same options, although not as extreme. These are not new concepts just new levels. We have job sharing, flex time, can work from home on occasion, come in late, leave early, etc. as long as it doesn't adversely affect performance. Presence in the office is warranted most of the time to avoid additional costs and coordinate information in groups, but not required all the time. This level of flexibility should be a PRIVILEGE (for the proven), not a RIGHT" (emphasis his or hers).

Privilege is a funny word, isn't it? Isn't that a word we use with children when we feel the need to remind them who's in control? Do your homework, young man, or no Xbox. Video games are a privilege not a right!

According to *sheezheer*, the ideal state of work is still in the office, in meetings, in the physical space. In other words, we're back to the idea that because a company owns the product of your work they also own your time. They have control over where you are and when. A little flexibility is okay, but too much flexibility is "extreme." You need to be remarkable to be treated like an adult.

We're also back to the Flexibility Con Game. In fact, as the following table shows, one way of defining a Results-Only Work Environment is by showing what it's not. Because it's definitely not flextime. In a ROWE employee control isn't a perk—it's the norm.

Flexible Work Arrangement	Results-Only Work Environment
Permission required	No permission needed
Limited options—inflexible	Unlimited—fluid
Management controlled	Employee managed
Requires policies/guidelines	Requires accountability/clear goals
Focus on "time off"	Focus on "results"
High demand/Low control	High demand/High control

There's a misperception out there that just because a manager lets an employee go to a dentist appointment, then that's flexible working. That's not flexible working at all. ROWE is really putting the freedom and the power back in the employees' hands to determine what and how and when people work best. A Results-Only Work Environment is about recognizing and acting on people's need to have more control over their lives to meet *all* the demands in their lives.

In other words, no matter how flexible a nontraditional schedule is it's still a schedule. *Flexible schedule* is an oxymoron. Which is why in a ROWE there are no schedules.

So how can this possibly be? Not that anyone wants Sludge, but what happens when the status quo starts to break down? If I'm not playing time games with myself and other people anymore, if I'm really free to do whatever I want (and you are—this is not a trick), then how do I measure my performance? How does my manager judge my work? What am I supposed to be doing with my time?

These concerns are addressed by the second half of the definition of a ROWE: as long as the work gets done.

"As long as the work gets done" is no small thing. As we

said in the last chapter, a Results-Only Work Environment is not about working less or making work go away. Those five projects? You still have them. But instead of measuring your performance based on the outcome of those projects plus a sprinkling of face time, getting in early, and kissing your boss's ass, you are only measured on results. If you do a good job then you are rewarded and paid and promoted based on the job you do and nothing else. We've arrived at Phil's idea of getting real with what you can do and then intensely focusing on business results.

There are going to be skeptics who will say that their workplace is already like this. We're certainly not claiming that we invented this idea of basing work on results. There are a lot of companies that are mostly focused on results. There are managers within larger, more rigid companies that look the other way on hours as long as people focus on results. There are even professions—such as sales—that allow almost complete autonomy for their workers as long as they meet their monthly numbers.

But we would challenge any business in terms of how thoroughly they embrace a results-only approach. Does the organization even in a small way still reward (or punish) people based on time? Are there core hours? Or if you aren't performing does your manager suggest you put in more time? Or do your coworkers judge one another based on the clock? Furthermore, does *everyone* in the organization work in a results-only model?

What's tricky about these beliefs is that we often don't know we have them. Once wc were speaking to a group of high-level people in a Fortune 100 company. To demonstrate how pervasive the unwritten rules of a culture are, and how they are a part of a larger cultural system of work, we asked them what time was considered coming in "on time."

Because they knew about ROWE they had already anticipated our game. They said, "We can come in any time." Some of them were even kind of smug about it, as if to say, See, we're flexible.

But then we asked, "Can everybody at your company come in whenever they want, just like you?" This sobered them up and they then admitted that not everybody could come in when they wanted to. When we asked again what coming in on time was, they all knew the exact time to the minute. The same was true for what was considered leaving "early." Because they were high-level employees the rules may not have applied to them (they'd "earned" freedom and trust), but it certainly was the unwritten rule of the culture to mind the clock or suffer the consequences.

A Results-Only Work Environment is companywide. At Best Buy, ROWE is not for the top performers or the directors on up, nor does it disappear during the busy season. It's for everybody, all the time. It's the focus of how work gets done.

In a ROWE, you stop paying people for activities and start paying them for outcomes.

In a ROWE, you stop paying people for a chunk of time and start paying them for a chunk of work.

"As long as the work gets done" is an absolute. The employer's job is to create very clear goals and expectations. We're not talking about job descriptions, which quite frankly only provide the most basic expectations for what an employee is supposed to do. We're talking crystal clear expectations for what needs to get done on a daily, weekly, monthly, and yearly basis. Then it's up to the employee, with the coaching and guidance of management, to meet those goals and expectations. If problems or challenges arise along the way, it's the work—and not hours worked or the perception the employee is creating—that comes under scrutiny. Employees are expected to bring their full powers to accomplish their goals. Employers trust that the work will get done. Anything that is not related to the task at hand falls away.

This idea of only focusing on getting the job done has an enormous ripple effect.

For example, one question we often get when we talk to people is what happens if someone gets their job done in thirty-six hours rather than forty? Is there an obligation to ask for four more hours of work? Or should the manager then give that person four more hours of work?

The answer is neither because you're not judging performance based on time. You are only rewarded based on outcomes. As a result, in a ROWE you approach work differently because rather than being punished for getting your work done more quickly or more efficiently, you are rewarded.

The right question to ask yourself in a ROWE, when you're at the halfway point in your week or your project or your day, is "Am I doing what I need to do to meet my goals?" If the answer is yes, then you're on track. If the answer is no, then you start asking yourself, "What do I need to do?" It's like the countermove to Sludge: Ask yourself what needs to get done. If you're focused on the results and achieving them then your time is your own. You got it done in thirty-six hours? Good for you! Dress up in Renaissance fair clothes. Take your kids to a movie. Save the world. You did your job. No one cares how you spend your time.[*]

---

[*] A ROWE is slightly different for hourly employees in a corporate setting.

We realize that this sounds like free ice cream being served on golden platters by magical fairies. Often when we first introduce this idea to people they say that being able to do whatever you want, whenever you want as long as the work gets done is a lovely idea, but it could never happen where I work. They say that even if working this way were possible, there is no way any organization—especially my organization—could make such an enormous change. As appealing as this idea is it just doesn't seem possible. It's hard to imagine some anonymous dude in a suit with a rolling bag coming into a conference room and teaching this new way of working as if it were time management tips or sales techniques.

This much is true: A Results-Only Work Environment cannot be created in the traditional way. A man or a woman with a rolling bag can *start* the process of transitioning from a traditional workplace to a ROWE, but they cannot force an organization to adopt this mind-set.

At the same time, you would be surprised what people can do and how much they're willing to effect change if

---

Hourly employees don't have work schedules, and they are still free to do whatever they want, whenever they want, as long as the work gets done. So they might work for an hour at ten at night, or from home for all or part of the week. They have schedule control. Unfortunately, because of Department of Labor regulations, nonexempt employees still have to track time in order to get paid. We think this is stupid and outdated. Having to track your time even when you're delivering results makes people feel like second-class citizens. It's not good for people, and, in a knowledge economy, it's not good for business. We believe that eventually the Department of Labor is going to have to change its laws to catch up with the new realities of the global economy, but for now this is how nonexempt employees experience a ROWE.

given the chance. Because one thing is undeniable about a Results-Only Work Environment: A lot of people would like to work this way. They would like to be judged on performance, not politics. They would like to have more freedom over their jobs and to give their coworkers or employees more freedom to do their jobs. So the question becomes, How?

At first blush transitioning from a traditional work environment to a Results-Only Work Environment looks daunting. Given how change normally happens in corporate America, you can imagine hours and hours of training, piles of overproduced handouts, e-mail reminders from management to make sure everyone is on the same page with the new way, and so forth. In other words, not worth the trouble.

In fact, just the opposite is true, and to give you an example of what moving into a ROWE is like we offer the following story about litter.

As you know, there was a time when it was perfectly okay to finish your soft drink and chuck the empty soda can out the window of your enormous car as you sped down Route 66. In the middle of the last century everyone littered because it was socially acceptable to do so. Then, in 1953, the environmental organization Keep America Beautiful formed, and after years of flying under the radar as a large, but largely ignored, community cleanup organization, they created the famous "Crying Indian" public service announcement. Coupled with the Woodsy Owl "Give a Hoot, Don't Pollute" campaign launched by the USDA Forest Service in 1970, the Keep America Beautiful campaign helped turn public opinion around. Obviously people still littered (and they still litter today) but a lot of people stopped. And not only did they stop but they taught, encouraged, and sometimes harangued other people into not littering. Drop a popsicle stick in the street today and you may get away with it, but chances are you're going to feel bad.

This simple change in opinion has had profound effects. We wouldn't have Adopt-a-Highway programs without this change in people's attitudes. We might not be having as robust a discussion about the environment as we do now. We wouldn't have troubled teens doing community service in orange jump-suits by the side of the road. Or kids getting on their parents' case about doing a better job of recycling.

In the case of litter, the PSAs were the catalyst, but it was up to the culture to adapt to the new way of thinking. No one putting those ads on the air back in the early seventies could have envisioned where we are now. Nor could they have scripted it. But they did have a vision for how people should treat the environment and it started with something simple and doable and grew from there.

This is the nature of adaptive change. You start with a de-sired goal, then work your way toward that goal, regardless of where that process might take you.

Adaptive change is not what you typically find in corporate America. What you typically find in corporate America is technical change. Lots and lots of technical change.

Technical change is when the guy with the rolling bag comes in and teaches you tips and tricks and hints, but doesn't challenge the core problem your company is facing.

Technical change is when you are presented with the flavor-of-the-month management technique and you're sup-posed to pretend that it's not going to be a distant memory in six months.

Technical change is when management praises this exciting new program for its employees, but management doesn't have to change.

This is not to say that technical change doesn't have its place. When you have a new benefits program and people need to know about how this program will change their compensation package, then technical training is completely appropriate. The new rules fit on a handout. They can be articulated in an e-mail. You can have an orientation meeting to give people the facts. And the reason these kinds of techniques work for something like a new benefits program is that the typical corporate policy doesn't ask people to challenge how they behave.

ROWE, on the other hand, requires adaptive change. People have to act differently under this new way of working. You can't put the changes that occur for people in an e-mail because a ROWE works differently for each person, each team, each division. It's an ever-evolving process.

In fact, a key moment in the creation of a Results-Only Work Environment happened back before the Alternative Work Program pilot was implemented. Cali was assigned a change agent to make AWP happen. Cali and the change agent looked to other companies and steered the project toward examining best practices at other companies that were using flexible work arrangement programs. They created a lengthy guidebook about how to copy other programs. But the division leader of the AWP pilot didn't want to see other people's best practices. At one particular meeting he picked up the guidebook and said he never wanted to see anything like that again. He explained, in no uncertain terms, that this would be an organically grown movement that would not be dictated by best practices from other companies. Shortly after that meeting, the Human Resources representative removed herself from the project. Later, when Jody came on board, the focus was intensified on adaptive change.

The rejection of best practices was an important moment because from this point forward we were committed to real change. It was at this point that we had permission to disregard a solution that was comfortable and palatable. Instead we were committed to figuring out what people really needed and wanted and what was best for them. We were able to avoid the problem with so many changes in corporate America: They are fake changes; they are the flavor of the month. They look good and sound good and they seem to be addressing the problem, but they aren't and they don't.

Trying to create technical change for what is a social problem is usually a disaster. For example, before ROWE, employees complained about being in too many meetings. People said they couldn't get their work done. People said they were stressed and unfocused. People needed relief.

So someone proposed technical change in the form of No-Meeting Wednesdays. On Wednesdays you were not to schedule any meetings. The idea was that Wednesday would be the day when people could catch up on the work that they couldn't do the rest of the week because they were in too many meetings. The company invested time and money in training people on No-Meeting Wednesdays, promoting No-Meeting Wednesdays through flyers and e-mails, and even, of course, having meetings about No-Meeting Wednesdays. Then they rolled out the program. Problem solved.

Well, you can guess what happened. Abruptly cutting out Wednesdays as a day to meet was not as easy as it sounded.

Naturally there were times when people genuinely needed to meet on Wednesday. So when those people did so they were violating company policy, putting more stress on employees, and making people feel cheated out of their time.

So what did the company do? They trained people on how to have a really short meeting if you simply had to have a meeting on No-Meeting Wednesdays. So that meant only six PowerPoint slides to keep things short, but then they had to train people on how to give short PowerPoint presentations because that's not always easy, and so on and so forth. Halfway through the program there was more time spent training for, and in meetings and conversations about, making No-Meeting Wednesdays work than the time people were spending meeting on Wednesdays.

Also, just because people had their Wednesdays free didn't mean that there were any changes to the overall culture of meetings. True, you could get more work done on Wednesdays, but the work done on Wednesdays didn't look like work the way a day filled with meetings did. Nothing looks like work like a meeting, so people felt as if they weren't getting credit. For the more politically minded, not having meetings to schedule or to cancel out on meant they couldn't work on their image as a playmaker. They longed to cancel out on meetings or send a proxy to show their power and importance.

And then there was the guilt. People felt guilt for breaking the rules by scheduling meetings on No-Meeting Wednesdays. Guilt for not knowing what to do with themselves when they didn't have meetings. Guilt about thinking about this stupid idea in the first place as opposed to getting some work done.

Why can't we sustain this kind of change? We can't sustain this kind of change because programs like No-Meeting

Wednesdays can't possibly address the root problem. No time-management seminar is ever going to solve the problem of people not having control over their time. A seminar can give you tips and tricks. What people need is power.

What a ROWE requires, as we'll see in the coming chapters, is adaptive change. Adaptive change means that people's underlying attitudes and beliefs change along with their behaviors.

Think about TiVo. TiVo has to do with watching your favorite shows at any time. What TiVo gives you is control. You watch TV on your own terms, without commercials (or with, if you're into that), when you want, with whomever you want. TV is no longer on the network's terms (Must See TV Thursdays) but on your terms (I'll watch your show whenever I damn well please).

So people think about TV differently. They sample more. They hoard and store multiple episodes so they can watch them in batches. They might watch a late-night TV show only for the interview segment or only for the opening monologue. The key here is that no one tells people how to behave with TiVo. There is no right or wrong way to watch TV on your own terms. Rather, there is a tool that gives freedom, and then people figure it out for themselves, and they do it not by reading a TiVo instruction book but by experimenting with what works best for them and also by networking with other TiVo lovers to find out how to optimize their television-watching experience.

Another way of thinking about a Results-Only Environment is that it's a TiVo for your work. You give people the power and the control over their time. You also give them the ultimate in accountability: Meet expectations or you're in trouble. As long as everyone in the organization commits to these two ideals, then the change that results will happen organically.

We're not going to lie. Adaptive change isn't easy. While you're going through this kind of change the future state is being discovered. You are moving into an unknown, even if it's an intended unknown.

When adaptive change happens some level of distress is inevitable. Real change usually involves loss. People have a tendency to become comfortable in their habits, attitudes, and beliefs. When they are required to "lose" those closely held beliefs, they are inclined to grieve, struggle, and avoid the hard work required to adjust. But if adaptive change is to take place, they must endure the examination of their beliefs and open themselves to the reforming of those beliefs.

We understand this sounds big. Management naturally freaks out about this. They can feel their control eroding. But even regular employees have concerns about this. It's change. Change may be good but it's also hard.

One thing that might be reassuring is that an entire corporate population went through this transition and it worked. Also remember that people at all levels have the same worries.

How are the results going to happen?
How do we know we're achieving our goals?
How will we know that everyone is pulling their weight?

The glib answer is: How do you do that now? Because the way the game works now doesn't provide answers to these questions. Do you and your boss have clear meaningful discussions about expectations on a regular basis? (The semiannual performance review is a start but not enough.) Do you have a mechanism in place for determining if the daily work that's being done is driving actual results, or is it assumed that if everyone is there working hard then we must be getting it right? And finally, don't you personally know someone (and maybe it's you) who isn't pulling their weight or who gets credit where credit isn't due?

Before we started the pilot program for ROWE we polled managers on their concerns about all kinds of flexible work arrangements. Their concerns are the same ones we hear about a ROWE. They are also the same worries that a lot of employees have about work in general.

Is it fair?
Is there accountability?
Is there career development?

We took these concerns seriously. In response, and also to give ourselves a tool to measure our own results in making this change, we developed what we call a culture audit. Before we would migrate a team we would first poll everyone involved to try to understand how they viewed the nature of their immediate work culture. The questions are designed to take a quick snapshot of how work gets done and what work looks like in a given team or department. Did people think the culture was proactive or reactive? Did they think the organization was open to risk or afraid of change? Did management reward people based on face time or actual achievement?

What we've found across the board at Best Buy is that this survey trends toward the positive after migration. So even teams that score pretty well on people working effectively and with engagement see improvement thanks to ROWE, while teams that score negatively are profoundly transformed. Even taking into account the slippery nature of self-report, we feel confident that ROWE is making a difference.

As we move into the next three chapters we hope to show how these changes happen. And, as we'll see, despite a ROWE's seemingly radical approach, work actually ends up looking pretty much like it does now. People still go to meetings. People collaborate and team up. People are reachable. People are doing their jobs. Because that is what most responsible adults want to do. They want to do a good job and they want to be paid for it.

One final thought before we watch a ROWE in action. It's easy to see this idea in terms of employer versus employee. If employees get more freedom then the employer must lose out somehow. Someone has to win, right?

So, if you have to think about it in terms of one side having to win, we will be honest. The employee wins. The employee gets their life back, their sanity, and their sense of self-worth. But the funny thing is that once employees experience a ROWE they don't want to work any other way. So employees give back. They get smarter about their work because they want to make sure they get results. They know that if they can deliver results then in exchange they will get trust and control over their time. And once they are trusted with their time, they will fight to keep it that way.

Voices from a ROWE: Trey

Trey is an e-learning specialist. He is an individual contributor who does not manage people. Trey is in his late twenties and has been in a Results-Only Work Environment for almost two years.

When I was in college the mood on campus was that all corporations are inherently evil. While the bulk of this hatred was focused on companies like Wal-Mart and McDonald's, the overall atmosphere was very anticorporate. Having never worked for a corporation, my perspective of corporate America was also very negative. When I told my friends I landed a job at Best Buy's corporate headquarters they basically said that I was bowing down to The Man just to make a buck.

Once I started working for Best Buy and got into a Results-Only Work Environment my view and the views of my friends eventually changed. When I told friends and family I had the opportunity to work when I want, wherever I want, at first they didn't believe me. As time passed and I had story after story of my incredible experiences with ROWE they began to change their minds. Their overall view of "corporate America" hasn't changed, but their view of Best Buy's corporate head-quarters has definitely changed. My employment opportunities and lifestyle are now envied within my social circle. I don't hear about evil corporate America from people anymore. Instead people say, "I want your job."

When I compare my life two years ago, working a steady eight-to-five role, with where I am today I can't help but smile. In my eight-to-five role there was no flexibility. I had two weeks of vacation time and a fixed amount of sick time. Because there was no flexibility, I had to use vacation time to go to the dentist or the doctor. Leaving early or coming in late resulted in disciplinary action. I recall the hassle I had to go through to take three weeks off to follow my favorite band. I ended up using all of my vacation time and taking a week's "leave of absence."

I think the best way to compare life in a fixed eight-to-five role with what it's like to work in a ROWE is to just describe my life the past year. For the most part I am able to get up when I want and choose when and where to work. There are times when I need to attend meetings or get work done in a pinch, but those instances are few and far between. Some days I will feel like heading into the office; some days I won't. The past month I have been in the office before ten probably two to three times, and only because I had a meeting.

A typical day for me includes waking up when my room is too bright from the sun and I can no longer sleep. I check my e-mail to make sure there are no pressing issues and respond to anyone who needs my input. I will typically watch an episode of *South Park* on the Internet, then walk to my local grocery store and buy some breakfast, even though it's closer to lunch at this point. After eating I will work in front of my television with ESPN on in the background. At this point I will choose to go into the office or continue to work from home, or maybe not even work at all and go for a bike ride or jog. If there is still work to do later that night, I'll do it then and it's no big deal.

I'm never *not* accomplishing anything. I always do what is expected of me. Because of the ROWE our team has gotten smarter about how we work. It used to be that one person would manage everything for a project and perform all the functions. We moved to more of a studio approach. Each person works according to their strengths. One person does copy. One person does Flash. I upload and implement and ensure functionality. Before we started working in a Results-Only Work Environment we could do ten, maybe twelve courses a month. We recently put forty-three courses out in a single month. This doesn't change when I travel. If I have eighteen projects going at once, I just set my goals so everything is done three days ahead of time, so I have a buffer zone before I hit the road. As long as the work gets done my manager is happy.

Contrast what I have just described with the eight-to-five life I lived a couple of years ago. While my friends sit in traffic and work a traditional lifestyle I work at my leisure from my apartment, or not at all, depending on how I feel and what I have planned for the day. This year alone I traveled through Europe for nineteen days following my favorite artist from Paris to Brussels, Amsterdam, Prague, and Cologne. I have a picture of Dave Matthews and me outside a small club in Brussels, Belgium. I spent a weekend at Taste of Chicago playing cribbage and Frisbee in a park, and capped the whole experience off with a show on Sunday night in the Windy City. I woke up that Monday in Chicago on a workday without a worry in the world. My only concern was if I was going to make it back to Minneapolis in time to go the Best Buy Charity Classic to see Dave Matthews for the second night in a row. This past weekend I took Friday and Monday off and had a weekend getaway with my girlfriend. We camped in a state forest and went to the Alpine Valley Amphitheater to see her favorite band, Nickelback. I spent Sunday at Noah's Ark water park cruising down waterslides. I will be in Chicago again for Lollapalooza and back at Alpine Valley for another show in a group camping site with forty friends from all over the United States.

None of what I have just described would be possible in the old work environment that helps create the perception of "Evil Corporate America." I basically do what I want, when I want, all the time. I do my work, for the most part, when it is convenient for me. Since I always get my work done I can enjoy life to the fullest while working for a great company.

CHAPTER FOUR

What Time Feels Like in a ROWE

B y 2005 ROWE was reaching critical mass. There were enough people working in a ROWE that it was getting harder and harder for anyone at any level to ignore the change, even if the idea still made them (or their manager) uncomfortable. Our presentations of ROWE, both to upper-level management and to the teams we were training, had evolved, and we were pretty secure in our ideas and our methods. The calendar exercise was gone. We were spreading the word about time, belief, and judgment. Sludge sessions were now a little more structured and focused. (Rather than asking people to come up with Sludge, we would offer them common Sludge phrases and ask them to explore their hidden meanings.) And we had arrived at our definition of a Results-*Only* Work Environment.

The only thing that we felt was missing was a set of guiding principles for what life was like in a ROWE, so one day we sat down and wrote the 13 Guideposts for a Results-Only Work Environment. This set of statements came from our sessions with employees at all levels, and they were designed to serve multiple purposes. First, they had to flesh out the basic definition of a ROWE so we had something to give people in addition to "You can do whatever you want, whenever you want, as long as the work gets done." Second, we wanted people to have a handful of statements that they could refer to as they went through the adaptive change process. If ever they were feeling lost when trying to make a ROWE a reality, they could look at the Guideposts. Third and perhaps most important of all, we wanted to shock people.

As we've said before, even if you get rid of the old attitudes about work, you need a new set of attitudes to take their place. You need a new culture. Making this happen means that every employee goes through what we call a migration process. The migration process does not involve training. People do not sit down with workbooks in a conference room for eight hours and study ROWE. Instead, ROWE facilitators introduce the same ideas you've encountered in this book—how time has a strange power over us, how we all labor under counterproductive beliefs about how work gets done, how we're all brought down by Sludge, how results and not time is the new boss. Then we turn people loose to make the change happen.

The 13 Guideposts needed to be extreme so that people realized that creating a ROWE required a radical rethinking of work. We wanted the Guideposts to be big and bold so that people left their first session about ROWE (called a Kickoff) buzzing with thoughts and feelings and ideas about what this new way of working could mean. So when we rolled them out we presented the Guideposts all at once. Before we explained or discussed what each Guidepost meant, we wanted employees to simply experience them as a thought experiment. We asked people to imagine what life would be like if the following were true:

1. People at all levels stop doing any activity that is a waste of their time, the customer's time, or the company's time.
2. Employees have the freedom to work any way they want.
3. Every day feels like Saturday.
4. People have an unlimited amount of "paid time off" as long as the work gets done.
5. Work isn't a place you go—it's something you do.
6. Arriving at the workplace at 2:00 PM is not considered coming in late. Leaving the workplace at 2:00 PM is not considered leaving early.
7. Nobody talks about how many hours they work.
8. Every meeting is optional.
9. It's okay to grocery shop on a Wednesday morning, catch a movie on a Tuesday afternoon, or take a nap on a Thursday afternoon.
10. There are no work schedules.
11. Nobody feels guilty, overworked, or stressed-out.
12. There aren't any last-minute fire drills.
13. There is no judgment about how you spend your time.

We knew right away which Guideposts were going to get people riled up. Not wasting employee time or company time and resources is valid and useful and good, but the idea that every meeting is optional really sets people on fire. What if you got to decline a stupid meeting that you knew was a waste of time? What if you really had the power to do that? What would life be like?

If these kinds of statements were shocking to employees,

you can only imagine what it must have been like when we first rolled them out to senior leadership and management.

From the beginning, management was vital to creating this change. So that everyone can benefit from a ROWE, everyone has to participate, and even though this is a people's movement, we always made sure to have buy-in, or at least a healthy optimism, from the top.

Before a team starts their migration, there is a leadership meeting. They get the same ideas, but these ideas are communicated in a slightly different way because the change for managers is different from that of individual contributors and teams. And as you can imagine, the first time we introduced the Guideposts to upper-level management there were some people in the room who were very uncomfortable.

The first reaction from management in those early days was the desire to negotiate. The idea of no work schedules was fine, but every meeting optional? Surely some meetings still have to be mandatory, right?

There was one leadership meeting in particular that was a real turning point for ROWE. After that meeting Jody was approached by people in management who said the Guideposts absolutely had to go. We couldn't show these ideas to employees. We had gone too far.

Afterward we met and argued over whether or not we would be willing to rewrite some of the Guideposts, but every time we tried to soften one or remove one we realized that we were compromising the idea. If every meeting weren't optional then people would still be judged on what work looked like. If there were still mandatory meetings they could be results-oriented, but not results-only.

Shortly after that discussion we went back to senior leadership and held firm. We challenged them to think about their beliefs about meetings. What does that say—about your meeting's effectiveness, about its usefulness—if people only come because of your title or because it says "mandatory" in the invite? How much productivity are you getting out of them if they resent being there? Isn't there a better way of transmitting that information other than having people sit around a conference room table and listening to people talk? We even challenged them to think about their own meeting behavior. Did they always attend "mandatory" meetings? Or did they find workarounds based on what they knew really needed to be accomplished that day?

We ended up winning the argument, and from that point forward the Results-Only Work Environment was in its full form. We made the 13 Guideposts a standard part of the ROWE migration. People started using them to help self-correct their behavior and attitudes. They also started using the Guideposts to help other people make the transition.

Any kind of adaptive change requires both self-adjustment and support. It's like quitting smoking or getting in shape. You can give people reasons for better behaviors, but ultimately they have to make the decision to change on their own, and the people around them have to support the change as well. That's part of the power of creating a ROWE: no one goes it alone. When people migrate from a traditional work environment to a Results-Only Work Environment they push one another, they challenge one another, they support one another. Management is part of the process, but management does not drive the process. The people create the new culture.

In the next three chapters we'll explore each of the 13 Guideposts. Each one speaks to a different aspect of a Results-Only Work Environment. Some deal with time, others deal with the logistics of how work gets done, while a third group points to how life is different in a ROWE. We're going to use these Guideposts to give you a better idea of what a ROWE is and also how a ROWE functions and feels. (Remember that a ROWE isn't a theory—there are people like Trey living the way they want to live right now.) We'll also try to work through some of the common objections people have, the Yeah, But moments that everyone has when confronted with these new ideas.

First we need to deal with time. Our attitudes about time are perhaps the hardest obstacle to overcome because they are so ingrained we might not even realize their influence over us. Even if someone waved a magic wand and said, You are no longer judged based on time, you would probably still judge yourself based on time. You have spent so many years with a "lunch hour" that even if someone said, Take as long a lunch as you like, you are still going to check your watch halfway through your sandwich to see if you're taking too long. You're still going to look at the clock on your dashboard while driving in to work that first week in a ROWE because when the clock says 7:59 and you're still on the interstate the alarm bells in your head are going to ring "late!" You're still going to look up at the clock on your way out, or check the time on your workstation when you log out for the day, because that's how you've measured your day since you can remember. Time isn't going to give up its power over you without a fight.

In a ROWE time truly doesn't matter. But this can be hard

to remember, and even harder to internalize. As we've said before, part of the power of the status quo is that it doesn't have to do anything to reinforce its attitudes. It's self-perpetuating. So the Guideposts in this chapter are there to remind you that in a ROWE, there are new rules.

Here are the new rules about time:

- Arriving at the workplace at 2:00 PM is not considered coming in late. Leaving the workplace at 2:00 PM is not considered leaving early.
- It's okay to grocery shop on a Wednesday morning, catch a movie on a Tuesday afternoon, or take a nap on a Thursday afternoon.
- People have an unlimited amount of "paid time off" as long as the work gets done.
- There are no work schedules.

Arriving at the workplace at 2:00 PM is not considered coming in late. Leaving the workplace at 2:00 PM is not considered leaving early.

At the most basic level this Guidepost means that in a Results-Only Work Environment you focus on results not on the clock. The clock is no longer what you use to determine if you are working or if you're not working. There is no late or early, only getting your job done or not getting your job done.

We're not saying that now suddenly work doesn't take any time out of your life.

Just because your effectiveness at work is no longer measured by time doesn't mean that work no longer consumes time. As we've said before, you still have a job to do and while an insight or an idea travels at the speed of thought, the execution of anything worthwhile requires diligence, attention, effort, and time. So if you're not pulling your weight, then the people on the team and your manager need to hold you accountable. Just because you can no longer be late doesn't mean you can't be lame.

What changes in a ROWE is that you and your coworkers and your manager no longer have to pay attention to time as a measure of productivity. There is no longer that extra layer of concern to weigh you down or cloud the issue. You might look at the clock to see if you have an appointment or a meeting, but you're not looking at the clock and thinking, Okay, it's three o'clock now so I need to get this part of the project done by five because that's when work ends. The rest of the job will have to get done tomorrow when work starts at eight. Instead you might look at the clock and think, Okay, it's three o'clock so I'm going to leave now to beat rush hour, go home, work out and eat, and then tackle this project at eight and finish it up by midnight so the deck will be clear tomorrow for the next phase.

What we have traditionally called "time management" is also different in a ROWE. Think about the typical time management course in which you move around your tasks and responsibilities with priorities or quadrants or efficiency buckets or whatever. The problem with all of these programs is that they don't address the root problem, which is that work is supposed to start at a certain time and stop at another, regardless of whether or not this is best for the employee or the business. Typical time management programs are asking you to make do with limited control, when the only solution is total control. These programs are asking you to find freedom within a prison.

♀ YEAH, BUT . . .

"If somebody is going to leave at two shouldn't they mark it on their calendar?"

At first people think it's common courtesy to let others know where they are and when they are working. But think about it this way: If you tell someone where you are and what you're doing at two on a Tuesday afternoon, then you also have to tell them what you're doing at midnight on a Saturday. We say that as long as the work is getting done, then it doesn't matter. In a ROWE asking someone about their time is a personal question. As long as the work is getting done then it's nobody's business but your own.

In a ROWE time becomes something you truly manage . . . because it's yours. You stop playing games with yourself and your time (now I'm working, now I'm not working) and instead you focus on what needs to get done. When it gets done (as long as deadlines are met) is up to you. So if you wake up at five in the morning and have the solution to a problem, you work on it at five in the morning, without guilt or resentment, and then you might do something for yourself or your family from eight to eleven, also without guilt or resentment.

Your whole internal monologue about work changes because your sense of time changes. One common refrain we hear from employees after they've been in a ROWE for more than one or two years is that they do not think about time anymore. They come in at a different time every day. They have no concept of when they're working or when they're not working or how many hours they have worked or haven't worked. They are so focused on results that they literally can't account for the time.* And if you asked them how many hours they worked they would think you were being weird.

The entire work environment also changes. At Best Buy, for example, you don't see the five o'clock exodus that you see at most companies. There isn't that feeling at four forty-five that the horses are in the gate ready to sprint toward freedom. People come and go with confidence because they know they aren't being judged on time. You don't strut in "early" with pride or slink out "late" with shame.

This change takes some time and effort. If it's one o'clock and one of your coworkers shows up for the first time that day, at first it may be hard not to Sludge them. It's also hard to be the only person on your team who's in the office for an entire afternoon. You can't help but wonder if people who aren't present are using their time wisely. Managers can have an especially difficult time not Sludging based on the clock because keeping an eye on people (and the clock) was traditionally part of their job.

Letting go of the clock can also be difficult because we've traditionally used time to measure fairness. If so-and-so gets to work a shorter day than I do, then so-and-so is getting preferential treatment. So-and-so is the Golden Child who gets to

---

*As we mentioned earlier, this is slightly different for hourly employees, who still track their hours in a ROWE. They may be more aware of time, but they do not feel oppressed by time. And because they have no work schedules and aren't tied to a desk, they do feel this increased sense of freedom and control.

do whatever he wants because obviously the sun rises and sets on his every move. And that's not fair.

But if no one can be considered late and no one can be considered as leaving early, then time loses its power.

> In a ROWE you don't use time to judge your own performance.
> In a ROWE you don't use time to judge your coworkers' performance.
> In a ROWE managers can't use time as a means of controlling their employees.
> In a ROWE control over one's time is no longer a perk for the select few.

The way to promote this new sense of time and to eliminate the old is through very open and transparent Sludge Eradication. In the beginning a lot of teams make a bit of a game out of Sludge Eradication. People call out their coworkers for Sludge and since it's everywhere every day, this can almost become a sport. "You're Sludging me, Jan!" and "I caught that remark about how long my lunch was, Bob!" Even though this sounds like a small thing, just the fact that anyone has the power to call out anyone else for Sludge based on time is a big deal. And as long as you're getting results you can wield this power without shame or embarrassment. Everyone knows that standing up for the work (and not tolerating discussions about time) is part of what makes a ROWE.

Any employee at any level can call out any employee at any other level for Sludge. So in those early days when people are still commenting on when people are coming and going, or bemoaning availability, it becomes extra important that people speak out, even if it comes across badly. Over time teams develop ways of monitoring their Sludge production in a way that's even and fair, and this often happens because over time everyone realizes that they are all guilty. When it comes to Sludge no one can stay on their high horse for long.

One final thought on this Guidepost: This new idea about time makes surprisingly deep changes in your work culture. Once you've eliminated the ideas of early and late, you start taking time out of the equation for every aspect of work.

For example, how long is a meeting? In most businesses a meeting is scheduled in increments of thirty minutes. But why? Maybe it's a function of calendaring software or maybe it's because when your mental framework is based on hours, then you naturally want to carve up time into neat increments. The problem is that this kind of thinking leads to meetings where you spend the time because there is time to spend. You allotted a half hour so you'd better fill it.

The other funny thing about time and meetings is that you are generally expected to attend a meeting from beginning to end. Only upper management has the right to dip in and out of the meeting, but for the rank and file your butt had better be in that seat and your bellybutton had better be touching the edge of that conference room table from start to finish.

In a ROWE people don't look at time in that way. We'll talk more about meetings in the next chapter, but for the purposes of this Guidepost, in a ROWE you are free to use your time in a way that best drives results. As we'll see, meetings become negotiable and part of that negotiation involves time. Rather than sit through an entire meeting, you might show up for the first ten minutes to make your contribution. Your time is always your own.

It's okay to grocery shop on a Wednesday morning, catch a movie on a Tuesday afternoon, or take a nap on a Thursday afternoon.

If work teaches us how to do one thing well, it's how to make up really excellent excuses for not being there. By the time you've been in the workforce for three or four years you are, if anything, a black belt in excuse making. Everyone has their favorite excuses. Everyone knows to save the good ones for when you really need them. Everyone knows to rotate the old favorites or to put a new spin on them to keep the Sludger at bay.

There are also rules for excuses. If you're going to be late, then you're going to want to blame it on traffic, not on the fact that you were eating the most delicious pancakes you'd ever had in your life and it seemed a shame to rush a moment you'd rather savor.

So the status quo makes us masters of the white lie. But there is something deeper going on here, something that gets back to the idea that your job owns your time. If your job owns your time, then it is doing more than dictating how to use your time. Your job is also creating an alternate universe with its own set of rules that govern the socially acceptable and unacceptable uses of all this time that you don't own.

In a traditional work environment, socially acceptable excuses are the ones that you use to stop nasty comments. It's stuff like being sick, a doctor appointment, a funeral, a store visit to do competitive shopping, a car accident, a snowstorm, or even something as small as taking a personal call from your sick mother. If someone says, "Where were you yesterday?"

then noting that you were at the doctor's office or at a funeral is going to stop them in their tracks. You can't Sludge someone who has a "good excuse."

Socially unacceptable excuses are the truths about our time that in a traditional work environment we dare not utter. This is when your lunch runs long because you were getting a haircut or running some personal errands. This is when you leave early because you want to catch a movie or go to a ball game. If someone says, "Where were you yesterday?" you would never in a million years say you were at a baseball game or getting a haircut. If you're walking in late you would never say it's because you were hungover or because you honestly didn't want to come into work that day and the very thought of walking those halls filled you with such dread that you couldn't get out of the shower.

And yet, let's look at how much time both the socially acceptable and the socially unacceptable activities take. (We'll leave the hangover and the dread discussion for later.) A hair appointment or a doctor appointment might take about two hours each. A funeral or a baseball game might take half a day. Some things, like dropping off your dry cleaning, aren't any more time-consuming than a quick phone call. We're back to those fifteen minutes that seem so important, but probably aren't.

Here is one of the ironies of the workplace: We put so much emphasis on time and yet we don't have a very good handle on how long things actually take.

If you were to give your boss a choice between having you out of the building for half an hour running personal errands or in an hour-long meeting at which your need to be there was dubious, most bosses would probably pick the time-wasting meeting. Even if you could guarantee that nothing would get done in the meeting and that it might even run longer than an hour, many managers would rather have their employees in the building during traditional working hours doing nothing than out of their sight and being productive for their own lives. We would rather have everyone "present and accounted for" than "off running around doing whatever."

The reason is that the rules of work have more to do with enforcing how work looks than actually getting work done. We don't give people the freedom to run their own lives because they would take advantage, right? If we weren't all in the same building working, someone would abuse the privilege. They would be off doing something socially unacceptable with their time. If you leave people alone to do what they want to do then they will steal and cheat and fornicate like animals.

We've found that just the opposite happens. When people are in a ROWE they are actually more responsible rather than less because they are now being rewarded with freedom. What happens is that, rather than take advantage, people actually get more work done. Rather than people ignoring customers in favor of their own fun, they end up becoming more customer focused. Rather than acting entitled, they are humbled by the trust that has been given to them.

In a traditional workplace there is a line between socially acceptable behavior and socially unacceptable behavior. A ROWE erases that line. In a ROWE everything is acceptable as long as work gets done. And if the results aren't there, then that is what is unacceptable. Not your attendance or your tendency to be shy in meetings or your tattoos or your weird laugh. You don't get your job done and you don't get to keep your job. If you do your job you get freedom.

♟ *YEAH, BUT . . .*

"What if someone needs you when you're at the movies?"

The answer to this question is that you can't always reach people in a traditional work environment. Does it matter if someone is grocery shopping or at a meeting? Either way they're booked. The only difference is that in a traditional work environment being out grocery shopping is socially unacceptable. Furthermore, if there is a genuine emergency and only one person can help then that's a larger problem than one person's availability.

Teams start to work together more effectively as well. You get natural cross training and backup because everyone is benefiting from this freedom. As long as the goals and expectations are clear, people realize that if we take care of our customers then we have time for ourselves. People stop spending time and energy pretending to conform to their workplace's cultural norms and instead spend that time and energy doing their jobs. Rather than trying to look busy all the time or trying to look like good workers, they simply get their jobs done. They meet their customer's expectations instead of their boss's expectations about what work looks like.

This new attitude changes the workday. When any use of time is a socially acceptable use of time, people naturally expand the hours during which they are willing to work, even if they don't necessarily work more hours. We're back to the TiVo for your work idea. So someone might get up, answer some e-mails while they're still at home, then maybe run some errands in the morning (while keeping in touch via cell phone) and then come into work at ten and work until four, then go home, live their life a little, and then log on for an hour or two later that night. They're getting the same work done as if they got up, got ready, got to work at eight, and left at five; but instead some of the work happens before typical work hours and some happens after typical work hours.

That visit to the supermarket at nine in the morning instead of at the end of the day is key. When we remove the barrier between socially acceptable and socially unacceptable uses of time, then people have control over their lives. That balance between demand and control we talked about previously is restored. They are now getting things done in their lives and getting things done in their jobs, and the two don't necessarily feel that different.

The impact this change can have on people's lives can be huge. Some people use this Guidepost to do everyday things, like spontaneously going to the park with their kids. Some people use it to do remarkable things. One employee we know is using her freedom to go to graduate school. Rather than take classes at night over the course of many years, she is able to take classes and study during the day—during "normal" working hours—and as a result she can get her degree faster without sacrificing her job. Best of all, she doesn't have to give a second thought to how she's using her time. And she's an hourly employee, the type of person who in even the most flexible traditional work environment is chained to the clock.

People have an unlimited amount of "paid time off" as long as the work gets done.

Aside from flextime, there is nothing like a company's vacation policy to make people feel like crap. Take too much vacation and some department martyr is going to Sludge you for having too much fun while she logs in long hours of dedication and suffering. Take too little vacation and some department wiseass is going to accuse you of not having a life, of being an inhuman, workaholic drone who really needs to live a little. Take a vacation during a busy time and you're abandoning your coworkers in their hour of need. Take a vacation during a slow period and people notice that life goes on without you and question whether you are even doing anything in the first place. What should be a reward—what should make people feel good—is instead a huge Sludge generator.

Vacation time is also doled out in a way that reminds people of their place in the organization. Someone with a lesser position might have to earn their vacation hours based on a formula that takes into account hours worked. Rather than being recognized for your achievements you are rewarded for time in the chair. Meanwhile someone with a higher position might be lavished with vacation time on paper, but then privately reminded that no one above a certain level ever takes all their vacation. Then there are rules for when time off can be taken (please, no vacations in your first six months here) and how it must be reported (using Form V1295 and submitted a month before proposed time off and subject to management approval) and then that delightful practice of making it all disappear at year's end if you don't use it, as if someone cooked you a gourmet meal then pulled your plate because you weren't eating fast enough.

If someone in corporate America has taken a clean vacation (no guilt, no worry, no comment from their boss or coworkers) we'd love to hear about it. You could not design a more miserable, broken system. When it comes to vacation, you cannot win.

In a ROWE people focus on results, not how many hours they've logged on the books. Unlimited time off doesn't mean that everyone is on permanent paid vacation. As we've said before, you have more responsibility, not less, in a ROWE. You are responsible to your team members and your customers to get your job done. You can't stick your coworkers with your job while you hit the beach.

What unlimited time off means is that you are no longer rewarded with chunks of time. In a traditional work environment your job rewards you with hours that it doesn't own in the first place. In a ROWE your job rewards your results with money. Your time is your own to do with it what you please.

Time off is no longer a reward. Control over your time is the reward.

Just think about those two weeks off or one week off in the traditional work environment. People are so overworked and stressed-out that often when they finally do get a vacation they spend the first three or four days just freaking out over having that much time on their hands. The status quo robs

people of their control, and so when they do have total control over their time they don't know what to do with themselves. You can lose the ability to govern yourself. Or you
need so much time just to decompress that your vacation is
half over before you're really enjoying yourself and then when
it starts to draw to a close you get a colossal case of the Sunday night dread and you're miserable because you don't want
to go back.

In a ROWE people treat time off differently. For starters,
people don't feel the crushing need for vacation as acutely because they are working when they are most productive for
them and not working when it's least productive for them. Remember that a ROWE isn't a flexible schedule; it's the absence
of a schedule. So people take breaks in bits and pieces as a way
of managing their own energy. They might go really hard for
three straight days and then take it easy for a day, then work
hard again for another day, then take three days off. And the
best part is that you don't have to justify any of it. If you are
doing your chunk of work, then you don't have to explain your
time.

In practice this Guidepost means very different things for
different people. There are people in project-oriented jobs like
Trey who work like mad to get their work done for the month
in two weeks and then travel for the second two weeks of the
month, only checking in via cell phone and e-mail. They are
essentially on vacation for half the time. (They are also pulling all-nighters for the other half of the month, but that's their
choice.)

Even people in more process-oriented jobs can benefit in
a similar way. In a ROWE teams cover for each other, allow-

ing individuals to take unlimited time off, and they don't necessarily have to track their time off. Your coworkers are okay with you going to Mexico for two weeks, because next month you'll support them when they go to Dallas to visit their grandma.

There are also people who use this Guidepost to do something that's in between. We talked with a person who spontaneously left Minneapolis one Sunday and drove to Boulder, Colorado, to visit his brother. He didn't take vacation time. He didn't even tell anyone where he was until Wednesday. For three weeks he worked in Boulder and to hear him tell it, work wasn't that different. Between his cell phone and his laptop there wasn't any interruption in his work flow. The only thing that changed was that when he was needed in a meeting, the people scheduling the meeting had to find a room with a speakerphone.

There are no work schedules.

This can be a tough Guidepost, especially for management. We have years and years of precedent of upper management getting together and deciding what needs to get done and then individual managers sitting down and figuring out what jobs need to get done and by whom and when. Managers have their chess pieces (aka employees) and they move them on the board according to the latest process-improvement philosophy, or based on their years of experience, or sometimes even their gut.

Even employees, as much as they might complain about being under The Man's thumb, can appreciate a good work schedule. It takes away the uncertainty of what to do with their time, and it forces the attention on filling hours rather than achieving results, which can create stress of another kind. With a work schedule there is one less thing for an employee to figure out.

But that's the problem. Work schedules that come from the top down only take into account one person or one group of people's point of view on what needs to get done at

---

⏱ YEAH, BUT . . .

"What about complying with federal regulations?"

ROWE is a paradigm shift in the way we do work, and it may take time for the federal regulations to catch up with how people live and work in the global, 24/7 economy. Right now, for example, we have the Family Medical Leave Act, which covers things like maternity leave. We think this legislation serves a good purpose, but it remains to be seen how this kind of law will change because of ROWE. If someone had a kid and wanted to restructure their life a different way (other than being completely "unplugged" from work for three months), as long as the work got done they'd have that freedom in ROWE. What this would look like from a legislative standpoint is unclear. These kinds of questions apply to exempt vs. nonexempt employee status, what disability leave looks like, and so forth. As ROWE spreads, these are issues that we'll all have to work together to resolve.

work—management. When managers move their chess pieces around they are missing out on what those chess pieces might be able to contribute to the conversation about what needs to get done.

In 2005 we noticed an unfortunate but not surprising phenomenon during some of the migrations. We saw in some cases administrative assistants weren't coming to the ROWE meetings. When we started asking around we found that a lot of them assumed that this new way of working wasn't for them.

Fortunately there is a professional group within Best Buy just for admins. We went to their monthly meeting and listened. It was a pretty sad meeting. We found that many of them still labored under the old secretary mindset, that even though the company called them administrative assistants and professed that they were valued by the company, they still felt like secretaries. So we started challenging them. Do you really have to sit outside your boss's office and wait? What if they're traveling? Can't you have your phone forwarded? Don't you have the same remote access to the company's internal network? They all knew how to do these things, but they felt like they didn't deserve it.

We disagree, not only on a human level but on a business level. Even people in support functions can benefit from having control over their time. Everyone deserves to work freely. When you eliminate work schedules altogether, then all employees are forced to make good decisions about how they spend their time and how to meet the needs of the business in a fluid manner. This is just as true for the admin as it is for the executive. If you give people control over their own job, and if you give them clear goals and expectations, then they will figure out not only the best use of their time, but the best use of their energy as well. As we'll see in the next chapter, which gets down to the nuts and bolts of working in a ROWE, when you treat people like adults they will respond like adults.

Voices from a ROWE: Ami

Ami works in online promotions. She is an individual contributor. She is in her early thirties and has been in a ROWE for two years.

Sludge eradication can be hard at first, especially in those first couple of weeks, and with a superior even more so. I'm comfortable pushing back on my boss, but some people aren't at first, and so they might try to joke about it. Which I think is how some people deal with it. Which is fine as long as they're keeping it top of mind.

If you have a strained relationship with your manager before going into a ROWE it's going to be even more important to address that issue once you're in a ROWE. At the same time it should give people a platform to stand on. The company is supporting this. You have to be able to say, "In the spirit of ROWE I don't feel like you're allowing me to do my best work whenever and wherever I choose." It's hard at first because you're torn between the old and the new. What makes it easier is that you can stand up for value. I'm saying no to unnecessary work. I'm saying no because I want to add value.

A ROWE gives everyone the power to question value. It doesn't take long for you to realize how strange it is that we weren't doing this before. Why weren't we constantly questioning before? You have ten people in a meeting but only two people talking back and forth. Why am I here? Because I received an invitation. Outlook has ruined productivity. It's just a joke. So what if someone is quadruple booked? You used to think that person was important. But now you look at that person and wonder what kind of value could they possibly be adding?

Now we're in different places working at different times so communication sharpens. You get clearer about expectations and deadlines. And you are constantly figuring out the best way to work with one another, which is funny because you think you're doing that already, but you're not. That's the paradox of a ROWE. You used to think that we all have to get together to get this work done. Now maybe the answer is that we all have to separate to get things done. Then when we are together it's strategic instead of assumed. It's purposeful.

I think what the skeptics realize is that they're not losing as much control as they thought. Everything boils down to results and so managers have some control over what the results are going to be. But the employees don't need to be controlled as much as they used to. I am much more motivated now because I have more balance. I can say no to things that don't add value, but I can also layer on things that I'm passionate about. I can do a deeper analysis of our competition. I can do offers that are more beneficial to our group.

So the trust goes up because you see the results. If this just made people happier, if this were a perk or something that just made life better, then maybe you could argue with it. But this does make your life better *and* it also gets results. How can you argue with that?

CHAPTER FIVE

How Work Gets Done in a ROWE

As we said in the beginning, when we introduce the idea of a ROWE to people they fall into two camps. Some people can not only immediately see how this new way of working would be beneficial to all, but they can also see that a ROWE is relentlessly pragmatic. They understand that given enough trust and support and direction most employees will rise to the occasion and get their work done in a timely and responsible way.

Then there are those who envision the end of the world.

For the doomsayers, more employee freedom means less accomplishment. They can't imagine anything getting done. In their minds, even if work sucks, they think that at least the status quo affords some measure of stability and control. Without that control a business descends into anarchy.

By 2006 at Best Buy corporate headquarters, there were more people working in a ROWE than in a traditional work environment. At this point even if you weren't in a ROWE you knew someone who was, and most likely worked on a day-to-day basis with a team or department that had made the transition. And yet when we would do a ROWE migration session, there were still people who resisted. Even if they saw coworkers having personal and business success with ROWE, even if they agreed that the way we work now was less than ideal, there was always at least one person in the room who said it was a nice idea for someone else, but for *their* group or *their* team it would be a disaster. In their minds the work simply wouldn't get done.

At this point we think it bears mentioning one of the surprising truths about a Results-Only Work Environment: It's not that different.

What happens on a day-to-day basis at Best Buy now that almost the entire corporate headquarters is in a ROWE is largely the same as what happened before. People talk on the phone. People type things on their keyboards and that typing makes things happen on their computer screens. They have ideas. They meet. They collaborate. They execute strategies that help their customers, both internal and external. The day-to-day tasks at Best Buy haven't changed. The company's core values haven't changed. The way work happens looks different, but people's jobs are largely the same.

Still, a ROWE does require an adjustment in the way you approach work, and the next five of the 13 Guideposts help address what a lot of people want to know: Just how does the work get done? If people are no longer tied to the clock, if there are no core hours or paid time off, if they aren't judging one another and themselves based on time, then what fills the void? If every meeting is optional, does that mean people never, ever meet? How do you handle emergencies? How, how, how?

Here's how it happens:

- Work isn't a place you go—it's something you do.
- Employees have the freedom to work any way they want.
- Every meeting is optional.
- There aren't any last-minute fire drills.
- People at all levels stop doing any activity that is a waste of their time, the customer's time, or the company's time.

Work isn't a place you go—it's something you do.

Why do we have cities? Why do we have office buildings? There was a time when it made sense for people who shared a common industry to get together to share information and ideas. You needed financial districts and fashion districts and movie studio lots and towns built around the automotive industry because if people couldn't physically congregate then the work couldn't get gone.

But what about how work gets done today? Think about how much work today exists as data. Think about the millions of bits and bytes of voice data, e-mail data, visual data that flows in and around us in a typical day. It's mind-boggling just how much work gets done over the phone or via e-mail, with people we may rarely meet face-to-face, or even with people around the country and around the globe whom we will never meet. Even people who work in "old economy" industries like manufacturing or farming end up pushing around a lot of electronic data. Everyone is a knowledge worker.

The funny thing about work is that every day most of us go to a physical space to do virtual work.

We go to our assigned cubes and put our butts in our assigned chairs to send and receive e-mails that only
exist as electronic packets of information.
We talk on a phone attached to a cord plugged into a wall
so we can have conversations that are beamed via
satellite to people across the globe.
We work on a laptop that never leaves its docking sta-
tion.
We use the neurons in our brains to work with ideas that
will hopefully stimulate the neurons in other people's brains.

When you force people to be at a specific place at a specific
time every single day, they're not going to give their best. If
they have an idea outside the sanctioned time and place they'll
fight it back. And when they're at work at least some part of
them will wish they were somewhere else. Nothing stifles creativity and innovation like resentment.

In a ROWE, work isn't a place you go—it's something you
do. The work going on in your brain can happen no matter
where your brain is. When individuals and organizations embrace this idea, it frees people up to do their best work. Give
people control of their time and their jobs and they start to
come up with creative, innovative solutions to problems at all
hours and in all kinds of surprising places. In a ROWE, people work where and when they work best, which means less
time and energy devoted to getting to and from work and
more time and energy spent doing the actual work.

This means no more hour- or two-hour-long commutes.
Part of that time is now spent solving problems that arise out
of your work. The rest of that time is yours.

⚲ YEAH, BUT . . .

"I like having a regular, eight-to-five schedule. I like being able to show up, do my job, and then leave. I don't want to have to think about it too much."

One of the things that's nice about a ROWE is that it's scalable to different levels of ambition. If you want to work 8–5, go ahead. Or, for people like Trey, who want to follow their favorite band around as much as they want a career, a ROWE gives them the freedom and control to manage their life so they can put their hobbies on the same level as their job. As long as the work gets done, then that's your choice.

But if you're saying that you just want to show up and put in your time, then a ROWE is not for you. The true slackers (which, we've found, make up a very small minority) don't last in a Results-Only Work Environment. The good news for the rest of us is that a ROWE no longer lets those people hide in the organization or play the Presenteeism game. In most departments at Best Buy, involuntary turnover rates (i.e., people getting fired for not doing their job) went up after they migrated. On the other hand, voluntary turnover rates (i.e., people leaving for a different company) plummeted. People who are willing to do their job don't want to leave.

This means no more Presenteeism. If work is something you do rather than a place you go, you can't hide from your job anymore. If you're not meeting your expectations and accomplishing your goals, you no longer have the excuse of being "on the job" working hard.

This means more communication with your coworkers, boss, and upper management. You might think that having fewer people in the office all the time would lead to a breakdown in communication, but quite the opposite occurs. In a traditional workplace you don't have to be efficient in your communication with people because you can count on them to be there. You can ask vague, meandering questions because you know that if you don't get a full answer you can always stop by their cube later. In a ROWE you make the most of every interaction because you have to. You still can count on your team members' availability, but you can't count on just stopping by. You can't waste people's time like you used to and you end up being much more efficient about your interactions.

Employees have the freedom to work any way they want.

In a ROWE you no longer judge people based on their work style. You no longer assume everyone learns and processes information the same way. In a ROWE you put people and their skills first and the job second. As long as the work is getting done you don't worry about how (provided of course that people are still behaving in a legal and ethical manner and one that is in keeping with your company's values). You no longer judge individual work styles.

So if you think best when you're on your feet, then go for a walk. If you do your best work at night, then work at night. Or if you need the structure of a more traditional work schedule then work eight to five. It doesn't matter.

For some, the gut reaction to this idea is that people will be less efficient and focused if they aren't given structure. But the opposite occurs. It's one of those ROWE paradoxes. Give people more freedom and they respond not with less focus but with more. When people are given the control to meet their demands, they end up being more on point. One person we talked to said that she was far more objective now. She could play around and let the task stretch to fit her day, but since her time is her own, and since she gets to solve problems on her own terms, she gets right down to it. Even though her deadline might not be for three days, she and her team turn requests around in twenty-four hours because there is nothing to be personally gained by waiting.

♀ YEAH, BUT . . .

"Don't new employees or kids just out of college need to be around to 'learn the ropes'?"

A ROWE doesn't discriminate based on age, sex, race, or years of company service. Some of the people at Best Buy corporate who are in a ROWE are older. Some are younger. Some of them just started yesterday. As long as an employee receives clear expectations, then it really doesn't matter where they are in their life or their career. If they can do their job, then a ROWE works for them.

Another interesting side effect of a ROWE is that you get a new perspective on "problem employees": you know, the ones who aren't always chipper in meetings, or seem to get extra flustered when you stop by their office unannounced, or the ones who are socially awkward around people who don't speak the very specific language of their field.

In a ROWE those people can really flourish because instead of looking at *how* they're producing you instead focus on *what* they are producing. It's not that office politics disappears, but traditional office politics are less important because everyone is being judged on results. If you produce, then you produce. How well you do is measured by goals and expectations that are established and monitored throughout the year. (No more rewriting your goals halfway through the year to make them fit how your job is really going, and no more surprises come performance review time.) Night owls stop sleepwalking through the morning and morning people don't have to pretend they're still effective after three thirty in the afternoon.

This Guidepost doesn't mean that people never get back to customers in a timely fashion or that they never come into the office. You're never allowed to use ROWE as an excuse not to do your job. But if you want to work from a coffee shop or from home, or if you want to work on a Saturday night, or a Sunday morning, then it all counts. There is no more of that telecommuting judgment that says that if you're not in an office then it's not really work.

As we've said before, most people do come to the office most days. For a lot of people at Best Buy, the idea that they have the freedom to work whenever they want from wherever they want is something they keep in their back pocket. The point isn't the time so much as the trust. When a company commits to a ROWE, it is committing itself to results, but it is also committing itself to an unprecedented level of trust. For a lot of people, just having that trust is enough. They still work pretty much regular hours, but it feels different because they know that if they want to, if the demand in their lives arises, then they have the control over their time to act accordingly.

As a result people take ownership of their work. They are being paid for results so they start behaving like entrepreneurs. They feel like they have a stake in the business.

Every meeting is optional.

This is probably the trickiest of the 13 Guideposts because this whole idea threatens the very core of the status quo. You say this to some people and they'll look like they're about to have a fit. Every meeting optional? How will people communicate? How will they build consensus? How will they collaborate? *How will they get any work done at all?*

We could write a whole book about meetings, but the point of this Guidepost is not the meetings themselves but the assumptions behind the meetings, namely that the very act of meeting is a form of work. We say it is not. If it gets work done then a meeting is work. If nothing gets done then it's just an elaborate social dance, a fancy way of wasting time.

Our favorite meeting story comes from Phil, the hardcore Six Sigma black belt. He is all business. One day, before ROWE, Phil was unable to come into work because of a snowstorm, which in Minnesota is perhaps the ultimate in socially acceptable excuses. Phil had six meetings scheduled for that day that were canceled because everyone was having trouble getting to the office. When he returned the next day, four of those meetings were never rescheduled. One was resolved with an e-mail, another with a phone call. He had spent much of his "snow day" worrying about those six meetings. He was ready to drive in and brave the weather in order to have them. Now that he's in a ROWE he thinks about that snow day a lot. When an invitation to a meeting comes up or when he's thinking about scheduling a meeting he puts on his "blizzard goggles." Is this meeting really necessary? If there were a snowstorm today, would that meeting fade away, or could it be taken care of with an e-mail, or, would it in fact prove to have genuine value?

A Results-Only Work Environment gives everyone the power to question the value of a meeting. That means anyone at any level can question their need to participate in any meeting. An admin can question a VP. (This doesn't always happen, but it can and does happen.) In a ROWE you can question weekly staff meetings. You can question "mandatory" training. At any given point you are free—and even encouraged—to make sure that the way you spend your time (and the company's time) is productive.

This Guidepost does not mean that people get to decline all meetings, or that they can decline a meeting that drives an outcome, or that they can become disrespectful and out of control. The point is to give people the power and the opportunity to have a discussion about value.

We've all been in a meeting where there are ten people but only two of them are talking.

We've all had someone schedule us for a meeting simply because they could, because the power to schedule other people into a meeting is a way of exerting their power.

We've all heard people show their importance and value to

YEAH, BUT . . .

*"I don't want to get everyone up to speed individu-
ally. I just want to broadcast my message and be
done with it."*

First of all, look around the room the next
time you have a "mandatory" meeting. There is always someone missing for some socially acceptable
reason—illness, travel, etc.—so you rarely get everybody anyway. And even if you do you don't always
reach people. Some people get a lot out of meetings. Others are checked out. So there is always a
give-and-take in an organization as people cross-train
one another, cover for one another, and so forth. At
the same time, if you're the type of employee who
constantly needs to be brought up to speed, in a
ROWE you need to fix that. Part of getting results
means getting the information you need whether
you're in the office or not. There is a big accountability jump when people work in a ROWE.

the organization by crowing about how many meetings they
have to attend.

We've all watched as people have abused scheduling software like Outlook to override common sense.

So you put the results first. When an invitation to meet
pops up in a ROWE it's yet another opportunity to take part
in that constant, probing conversation about results. What are
the results we're trying to drive? How does this meeting at

this time with these people drive those results? Who really needs to be in this meeting? Does this meeting even need to take place or can we resolve it via e-mail?

When you hold a meeting in a ROWE, you have to be very specific about what the meeting is for, what people are specifically expected to contribute, what they are going to take away from the meeting, and how all of this helps drive concrete, articulated results. When you do schedule someone you have to say, "Here is what I need you there for. Here is how long it should take. Here is what outcome we should get." And then you have to give the person you're scheduling the chance to push back. They can say, "I hear you, but I'm not the right person." Or, "I can help you with that but what if I were to give you X and Y ahead of time so we can spend more time in the meeting collaborating rather than downloading information to each other."

What ends up happening in a ROWE is that the number of meetings goes down and the number of people attending meetings goes down, but collaboration and teamwork actually go up. The reason is that people are more engaged during the time they are together. People prioritize their work. They become focused on what they need from people. And you actually learn more about your teammates and business partners than in the past because you actively try to figure out how you work best together. One of the ironies of a ROWE is that when people have less time with one another they make those interactions more purposeful and meaningful.

This change in meetings culture comes very naturally to some people. They embrace it and welcome it and it doesn't take them out of their comfort zone. For others, not having as many meetings or being forced to question meetings can be more difficult. We have developed a culture of consensus-building and teamwork in corporate life that is very comforting to some people. There are those who like being the tenth person in the overstaffed meeting that only needs three people. They like knowing a lot about what is happening in the organization even if not all of it has anything to do with their jobs. They like to add encouragement (or discouragement) to the group. In other words, they like to meet.

But we would challenge people to look carefully at how effective meetings are.

Do you really need every team member's input to move a project forward?

Do you really need everyone in the organization to be "up to speed" on every decision?

Do you really have to *be* together to *work* together?

There aren't any last-minute fire drills.

Every corporation has its own internal language for bullshit. At Best Buy we talk about fire drills and drive-bys. Remember fire drills at school? You might have one a couple of times a year, and even if the kids goofed off the teachers took it seriously and people eventually got in line. You learned to move quickly and (our favorite phrase) "in an orderly fashion." Even though a fire drill was just a drill, it meant business.

Now fast-forward to a corporate setting. A senior executive suddenly needs a sales report outside of the regular reporting period. Or a director wants a quick update on a project that's not due for another month. Or the president is walking the floor and wants to find out what people are doing.

So what happens? Fire drill! When we first joined the workforce we fell for this false urgency. Then after six months you realize that very few of these requests are real emergencies. Often it's an executive whim, or the result of poor planning. Sometimes the request even goes away before you get a chance to respond. After a while, you can't tell what's a real crisis and what's a fake one. In the worst organization, the day is one big crisis as you scramble to make up for past mistakes, or to catch up on work you didn't get to finish because you were in a meeting about the last batch of work you didn't get to finish.

At the other end of the spectrum is the drive-by. Executive Jill can make mountains move with her last-minute requests. Peon Joe can't, but he sure can pop by your cube for "just a quick question." The result of the drive-by is the same. You stop the work you're supposed to be doing, redirect your energy and focus to Joe, take time to answer that question, and then have to change focus back to what you were doing. What were you doing again?

This Guidepost addresses planning and foresight. Think of it this way: If people are working in their own style, and not tied to the physical office, and questioning meetings, and working when it's best for them, then everyone has to plan more, and there need to be a lot of conversations about outcomes. You can't count on just popping by someone's cube for a quick answer to that question you should have asked a week ago. You can't hope to cover your ass by making a vague comment or two in the next meeting. You can't expect someone else to pick up that ball you dropped a month ago, which you haven't gotten around to telling anyone about. And you no longer have to bail out your boss for their lack of foresight.

It's not that there aren't emergencies, or that the workforce is static and unmotivated. What changes is that you are no longer in reaction mode all the time. You no longer create the illusion of working by taking care of an emergency that wouldn't have transpired if someone had just done a little planning. You aren't going to hear "I need this by five o'clock" because you have been communicating with your boss and your team members about when action items are due. You are no longer living in a world of unnecessary drama.

In practice this means a new way of interacting with your manager. It's up to you to have a solid relationship with them because you have to be able to communicate what needs to get done, what good looks like, and how check-ins are going to work. There is a more open dialogue in a ROWE, and those kinds of performance-review conversations you have once or twice a year in a typical job are the kinds of conversations you have every week.

Managers, on the other hand, are forced to take more of a coaching role than a supervisory role. As a manager your job is no longer to supervise, to sit back and wait for people to either succeed or fail. In a ROWE managers take a much more active role in their employees' success because if they can't communicate the goals and expectations then the whole system breaks down. You can't judge people on appearing to work; you can only judge them on the work they produce, so you'd better have a very clear idea of what work needs to get done.

For a lot of people this new focus on results and planning and foresight is one of the best parts of being in a Results-Only Work Environment. It means you end up playing fewer games with people; there is less political maneuvering and less time spent trying to make people happy in intangible ways. Instead you have a job to do and you do it, and when employees and managers are united in work rather than engaging in unhealthy internal competition, then it's just that much easier to do your job. Employees end up teaching one another about their respective jobs. Your coworker doesn't need to know what you're doing and how you do it 100 percent, but if you're not around they can at least speak to your process and your relative progress.

True teamwork emerges, even in a department filled with individual contributors. One department at Best Buy, for example, is staffed with hourly employees who used to be only accountable for their own work. Their job is to process orders within twenty-four hours. The process has to be accurate but also fast (the customer can't see a slowdown). Before ROWE people were processing about fifteen orders an hour. After ROWE productivity went up 13 percent, but even better, the quality went up. The reason is that people are no longer judged on personal performance. Because individuals are now working at all hours of the day, the entire team is accountable for the business results. As their manager says, "We share in the successes and we share in the failures," and this means more planning and more communication.

Getting your head around how to communicate in a ROWE takes time. One of the dangers of a ROWE is that people try extra hard to respect one another's time. This is good, but at first it can also lead to people being overly respectful. They don't pick up the phone even when the person they're calling is more than available by cell. Often people solve that problem by putting together a preference list for how they like to be reached. They may prefer an e-mail first, then their cell phone, then their work line, then their home line. There are growing pains at first, but eventually people find out a way to both get what they need from their coworkers and respect their time.

But ultimately a Results-Only Work Environment is not

a test of the employee; it's a test of the manager. A ROWE becomes a proving ground for the management team. Can they do their jobs communicating expectations and holding people accountable? Can they develop systems to get the information they need without doing it through drive-bys or fire drills?

As one Best Buy manager put it, it's about being "clear and crisp." Managers can't be uncomfortable getting negative feedback or getting push-back from their employees. Managers can't develop one person's career at the expense of another's. Managers stop managing and start leading.

People at all levels stop doing any activity that is a waste of their time, the customer's time, or the company's time.

When you take care of your life, do you develop overcomplicated processes for getting things done? Do you spend your free time coming up with systems and programs for buying birthday presents or making dinner or feeding the dog? Do you have regular family meetings to discuss whether or not people are doing their chores, what the status of those chores is, and what kind of outcomes those chores are expected to achieve?

Why do we spend so much of our business life talking about the business we need to take care of rather than simply taking care of it?

In any organization there is always wasted effort. There is always busy work. Because if you're basing productivity on the clock then people need to be busy for forty hours a week. If their actual job only takes twenty hours to do then we'd better give them another twenty hours of reporting. Surely there is a form out there to keep these people busy.

In a traditional work environment there is no employee incentive to do a job more efficiently because if you did manage to get your job done more quickly you'd still have to fill the hours. So people might, for example, slow down their work so their task can take up the socially acceptable amount of time. And while they may question the need to do low-priority tasks they would never stop doing them out of fear of being seen as not doing their job.

In a ROWE people automatically edit their own work and remove low priority tasks. Just as they have the power to challenge the need to attend a meeting, they have the power to challenge whether or not a piece of their job is the best use of their time or if it is even necessary at all. Suddenly in a ROWE everyone is an innovative thinker because if they can get their job done more quickly and efficiently then they have more time for themselves. As long as they can drive the results, they are rewarded with control over their time.

This doesn't mean that people get to skip a critical process or that they can do as little as possible to get by or to call something unnecessary just to get out of working. Instead it means that people take ownership of the work they do because they have the power to decide what is best for them. What is their best work style? What are their most productive hours of the day? How are they best able to contribute to the company?

People talk about the waste falling away as if by magic. But it's not magic—it's a focus on results. If you have a job description then you measure your performance based on that description of what you're supposed to be doing. But there is no incentive to challenge how you spend the time. If you have a clear goal then you can mentally test whether or not the activity furthers the goal.

Most important of all, when you give people back their time they treat it preciously because they own it again. As we'll see in the next chapter, that completely changes not only how work gets done, but also how work feels.

Voices from a ROWE: Javier

Javier is an individual contributor working in Best Buy's dot-com division. He is in his early fifties and has been in a ROWE for two years.

Recently, the SVP of my department asked me how I was doing with ROWE. I've always thought that ROWE was great, but it's taken on a new meaning for me now.

About three weeks ago, I received news that my brother had passed away. He lived in Indiana. The news of his death was obviously difficult to handle, but it had an added piece of stress. You see, my mother has Alzheimer's and my brother had been her main caretaker along with a helper who is with her on weekdays. So not only was I trying to wrestle with the sadness of his passing away, but I was immediately wondering how my mother would continue to receive the care she needs. I was completely overwhelmed, wondering how I was going to handle this. Quite frankly, I didn't know what I was going to do.

I e-mailed my team about what had happened and that I would be leaving for Indiana to attend the funeral. I didn't even go into the Alzheimer's issues. My coworkers wanted to help, and offered to take care of my work for me while I was gone. They said I could go back to Indiana, focus on my family stuff, and not have to think at all about work. This was a nice gesture, but I knew I wanted to stay connected with my job at Best Buy. I know a lot of companies think that when a family member dies, you "should" disconnect yourself for a while. In fact, some companies force you to do that. But in my case, I really wanted to stay connected to benefit both myself and the company—probably myself even *more* than the company. I knew that having this distraction of being able to work would actually help me cope with everything.

With that being said, I went home to Indiana for the funeral and took my laptop with me. I continued doing my work and was able to handle that in addition to my family responsibilities. I felt fine about doing both and continued wanting to do both.

I didn't use any vacation time while I was in Indiana. In fact, I didn't track any time off at all. Now that I'm on ROWE, tracking any kind of time off seems ludicrous. It's not about taking time off—it's about getting work done, however that happens. Heck, I even worked from the Philippines for a week and took no time off. My job was completed over the Internet, and many people didn't even know I was out of town. If I were tracking time off every time I was away from the office or took care of family responsibilities, I would have drained my time off bucket a long time ago!

My sister and I are now taking things week by week with my mom. For example, I'm going to Indiana this Friday, Saturday, Sunday, and Monday to care for her. I'll have my laptop and I'll feel great, knowing that I'm contributing to my company and caring for my mom. Before my brother died, the woman who cares for my mom on weekdays had scheduled a three-week vacation in September. My brother was going to take over her care during that time. Now that can't happen, but because of ROWE, I'm able to step in. I will be going to Indiana for ten days to care for my mom. I won't be taking vacation time because I'll be getting my work done.

If it weren't for ROWE, I don't know how I would be getting through any of this. In the old environment, I would have had to take time off for my brother's funeral and then probably had to take a leave of absence or even quit in order to care for my mom who lives out-of-state. That would have just added to my stress and my company would have suffered as well.

Aside from the situations with my brother and my mom, ROWE has done wonders for my business team. Our productivity is definitely up—everyone talks about that. We just crank through stuff—we're focused on the work and you just get through it. There's not a lot of BS anymore. There's no time for people who are playing political games. ROWE isn't about that—it's about getting your work done. Period.

In ROWE, it doesn't matter who is in the office. When I do come into the office, I never know who will be there and that's okay. When I do see people in the office, my feeling about them has changed. Now I'm genuinely happy to see them. ROWE has made my job not just a job, but something I really care about.

If I left Best Buy to go to a new company without ROWE, they would probably think I had a bad attitude. That's how you're perceived if you don't go along with the office politics and all the BS games that go on. Plus everyone watches the clock. It's about desk time. But in a ROWE, you're in a world where all that's accepted is getting your job done, so all that stuff ends. It's not about the petty stuff anymore. I've let go of that now.

CHAPTER SIX

Why Life Is Better in a ROWE

There is an idea out there, a kind of macho work ethic, that work is battle, that work is all-out war. The popular vocabulary about business is filled with aggressive, combative language—you scratch and claw your way to the top; you're in the rat race; it's a dog-eat-dog world out there. It's as if success isn't just about your own personal excellence but also somehow about vanquishing your foes.

Isn't that how it is? We say, Maybe.

We don't doubt that for some people business is a battle and victory feels like winning a war. And we're sure the true titans of industry must feel an enormous amount of power in making their decisions, and that when a hunch or a risk pays off it must be very rewarding.

But we say "maybe" to the whole business-as-battle idea, because while we admire the businessperson-as-warrior, and while we can celebrate the alpha- (usually) male entrepreneur, a lot of work frankly isn't that dramatic. For most people business is not a battle at all. There are no lands to conquer. Most people get up, go to work, and do their jobs with varying degrees of success. Most people don't need to have all the toys, or a mansion and yacht, or a profile in *Forbes*. They want to do their jobs, to be paid fairly, and to be left alone. They do not dream of the day that their competition's head is stuffed and mounted on their office wall.

Still, this business-as-war metaphor is interesting because of the attitudes about work that it reveals. It's also interesting because of what it allows people in power to do in the name of achieving business glory.

> Business as war means that there are an acceptable num-
> ber of casualties.
> Business as war means there is collateral damage.
> Business as war means people and ideas and sometimes
> even ethics are sacrificed.

What is done to ordinary workers in the name of business as war? The answer is Sludge. If we all accept that work has to be a certain way and feel a certain way, if we all accept that sometimes you have to make sacrifices (of your time, of your sense of fairness, of your sense of decency), then there is really no limit to what can be done in the name of work.

But we're not just talking about business ethics, about the decisions that companies and corporations make. While we believe that businesses should have integrity and ethics, this is not as much our concern as how people are treated and how they feel at work. We're really talking about changing the whole conversation about what work is for. It doesn't have to be a battlefield where a few people win (or lose) big. Work can be a place where everyone can find their level, their place, their sense of purpose. Everyone can be respected and valued, and not just because it's the humane thing to do, but because it makes business sense.

> Because when business is war, you don't have to respect people as individuals. Orders are orders.
> When business is war, you don't have to trust them. Everything is on a need to know basis.
> When business is war, people aren't really people. They are pawns in the chess game.

The sad fact is that our culture believes these attitudes about work are okay. Call it Sludge Resignation. People have no choice but to put up with the status quo. You can't fight City Hall. It is what it is. So we put up with feeling like we're at war all the time, and we sacrifice our freedom and the ability to feel good because that's what you have to do to get ahead. You lose your personality and your identity and your humanity. You take one for the team. Because if you don't, the thinking goes, then you don't have what it takes.

We find stories like Javier's personally gratifying. The idea that ROWE could be a real help to someone in their time of need makes us feel wonderful. At the same time, we didn't just offer his story as a feel-good testimonial about the power of ROWE. We also challenge you to ask yourself why work should be any other way. What would be gained, either on the human level or the business level, to punish Javier for having demands outside of work? It would be like punishing him for being a person.

There will never be a time when his story isn't uplifting and encouraging, but wouldn't it be wonderful if his story

were also the norm? We don't see this kind of gain for the
employees as a loss for employers. As Javier said, he and his
group have never been more productive.

Of course there are going to be winners and losers. There
is going to be success and failure. But we're not at war and we
shouldn't have to feel like we're at war just because we've gone
to work.

So these next Guideposts, while they deal with something
that seems squishy like feelings, are really the heart of a
Results-Only Work Environment. A ROWE doesn't make
your job easy, but it will make work not feel so hard. If people
don't feel free and rested and trusted then you don't have a
ROWE. Because the whole key to a ROWE is that the way
work looks and feels is completely different. It is not recognizable as work. It is something else, something better.

Here are the Guideposts that make it happen:

- There is no judgment about how you spend your
  time.
- Nobody talks about how many hours they work.
- Nobody feels guilty, overworked, or stressed-out.
- Every day feels like Saturday.

There is no judgment about how you spend your time.

This is the no-tolerance-for-Sludge Guidepost. One Best
Buy team, for example, didn't have a lot of dramatic Sludge
pre-ROWE, but even after migration it took time to get rid
of it entirely. There would be subtle things, like when people
worked at home they felt obligated to report everything they
got done. One time an employee was home sick but he wasn't
taking a sick day. He just pounded some Nyquil and got a ton

done, but people were joking with him about how much better he worked on Nyquil, that maybe he should get sick more often.

And his team leader stepped in and said that you really can't even joke about that stuff. Because even when people joke to test the limits of a ROWE it can have a ripple effect. Then other people start making comments and you can backslide. Jokes about time—even really, really funny ones—erode trust. These kinds of jokes are based on the assumption that ultimately it's really not okay to work and live this way.

This Guidepost doesn't mean that people are disrespecting management or that there is a total breakdown of company values or confusion or lack of direction. In fact the opposite occurs.

People show total respect for the work and the people doing it.
There is complete trust between employee and manager.
People are focused on the bottom line and only the bottom line.

Imagine how this feels. You are free from judgment about time. So you go into work and you do your job. If you have to get your oil changed at 1:00, you go do it. You have your cell phone with you in case someone needs you. But you don't even have to tell people that you're leaving. You don't have to make up a lame excuse. Because no one is judging you. If someone calls you and you're walking on the treadmill you don't have to say, I'm working out but I promise I'll be right back. You can say, What do you need? Answer the question, hang up, and not even think about it. (You may also opt to let the caller leave a message, just like you do when you're in a meeting.)

YEAH, BUT . . .

"You can't erase what's in people's heads. And you can't prevent people from saying mean things about people."

This is true. There will always be people who judge how you spend your time. However, in a ROWE you look stupid for letting those judgments come out of your mouth. Just as it's not okay to say something racist or sexist in a traditional workplace, it's not okay to judge time in a ROWE. Judging people's time is no longer socially acceptable. Even better, a ROWE actually gives you a mechanism for dealing with that judgment. So while in a traditional work environment the office lout can get away with saying rude things because he's the boss, in a ROWE if someone judges your time you always have Sludge Eradication. You may not have the power to stop people from acting stupid, but you do have the power to shut them down.

There isn't less judgment or more favorable judgment. There is no judgment. Zero. Frankly, people are too busy doing their actual jobs. There is so much to do. People can take work to a much deeper level than they ever did before because they are caught up.

It's an interesting feeling when you walk into the office and have no judgment about time. You also have no judgment about what good work looks like. Imagine walking onto a floor of an office building and seeing cubes that are filled, cubes that are empty, seeing someone walking along the hall, someone having coffee or leaving for the gym, people gathered in a conference room meeting, and people talking by the watercooler. Now imagine not being able to make any judgments about whether or not those people are being productive. The only way to know is by seeing if they are delivering results. You can't assume anything. You can't just look at a clock or whether or not someone's hair is wet because they've been swimming or maybe you haven't seen them for a week. You can't assume they're slacking or taking advantage in a ROWE.

So if you can't judge people on their time, what can you do? Often you don't do anything because it's none of your business. If you are getting what you need from people so you can do your job, end of story. So you simply don't waste that time judging.

Now flip it around. Imagine yourself walking into this kind of office environment and not feeling judged. You walk in at three. You have been gone for three days, still doing your job, from home or a golf resort, or the coffee shop. You walk in and people say hello and that's it. There are no looks, no rude little smiles, no eye rolls, no ostracism, no nothing. You don't have to anticipate any Sludge or ready a reason for why you've been "MIA" for three days or make up some nonsense about how hard you've been working to make up for the fact that you haven't been around. Instead you walk into a completely neutral space, because everyone is getting the same treatment. You're not judging them so they're not judging you.

So if people aren't judging you then what happens? You make sure that you're getting your job done. Because if you're not you're in big trouble. You're really going to stand out. You can't fake it anymore—you have to do your job. You have to communicate with your coworkers and your manager. You have to figure out how to make things work better and smarter and more efficiently. So you walk in at three and you do your job.

As we've said before, work isn't that different. It feels different. And having people not judge your use of your time and only judge your accomplishments is an amazingly liberating feeling. Enjoy your Nyquil.

Nobody talks about how many hours they work.

This Guidepost can be a real treat for a lot of people, because they now don't have to play a game they know they can't win.

You know that person in your office who brags about the marathon workweek? The one who you almost expect to show you their battle scars? Or the people who do this kind of fake complaining about how many meetings they're in? The ones who can't believe how many meetings they have and how they just don't have a minute to take a break from being so incredibly important and in demand? If they got any more necessary to the organization they would lose their minds. Or what about the vacation martyrs? Or the eat-at-the-desk martyrs? Or the I-don't-have-time-to-eat martyrs?

In a ROWE you never have to listen to that crap again. You get no extra credit for spending time. There are no time card heroes. No overtime heroes.

As one Best Buy employee put it, "If someone said that they worked sixty hours, the first reaction is, Who cares? The second reaction is, Well then you better show me sixty hours of rock-star work. Because that's all anyone wants to know about. What did you get done?"

In a ROWE, if you want to come in on weekends or stay late or come in early, people will assume that is your personal choice about your work style. They will not assume that you are more dedicated, more hardworking, more accomplished. In fact, if you really pile on the hours, it might even raise some red flags.

In a ROWE people will offer you tips for doing your job better.

In a ROWE your manager will try to help you make things more efficient so you can dig deeper into your job.

In a ROWE people will smile politely and ask you what you got done.

People in a ROWE sometimes describe this Guidepost in terms of clarity. When people aren't talking about hours or bragging about hours—when the business is not recognizing time but results—then things are clearer. Rather than measuring time and effectiveness in your job, you just measure effectiveness. Identifying and solving problems then becomes much simpler.

This doesn't mean that people milk the system or that there is no capacity planning. You can still talk about time. You can still plan around time. "I think this will take two weeks" or "we need to build in a month to make sure that happens." It's more a matter of not basing achievement on time.

This is not easy for some people. There are a lot of people out there who have based their lives and work identities on being the one with the iron butt. And there are people who need—or feel they need—to put in long hours to get the work done. Still, this Guidepost really puts the nail in the Presenteeism coffin. Isn't that what bragging about hours is really about? It's championing Presenteeism.

There is still, of course, a social aspect of work. One of the weak points of a ROWE is that people can start to feel disconnected. That's natural. So what people do is they make sure to take time as a team and as an organization to do social activities. It's not team building and it's not forced fun. Instead a team decides that it needs to connect on a social level and then figures out the best way to drive that result. When teams take this kind of action, it's far more meaningful than meetings for the sake of meetings.

It can also be hard for newcomers to enter a ROWE because it's a different setup. But again, once people realize that there is no pressure to be there, only pressure to get results, then the equation changes. Newcomers realize that they don't have to lie. They don't have to figure out the secret rules of the culture like pretending to be around or filling out a false time card or beating the boss to the office. Newcomers don't have to look busy. They can simply do their job.

This is true for everyone. Imagine talking with someone and the whole idea of hours worked never comes up. Let's say you're efficient and you can get your job done quickly. That's great. Then there is more time for you. What's amazing is that at first people really measure their hours worked. After a while, when you ask people how many hours they work they don't really know. They might be aware of their job being harder or easier, or it being a slow or busy time, but as that line between socially acceptable and unacceptable goes away, people aren't putting time into a work box and a free-time box. It's all their time. So they don't keep track. What they do know is that it's in their best interest to be smart and efficient about their jobs. Because the less time they spend delivering those results the more time they'll have to do their own thing.

Nobody feels guilty, overworked, or stressed-out.

Stress can do crazy things to a person. We talked to one employee who used to get so stressed-out coming to work that she would get in traffic accidents. Most of them were pretty minor but one time she ended up in a ditch on the side of the road. The only reason for this was that she felt compelled to be in on time.

Now she comes in when she feels like coming in. No more accidents.

You still work hard in a ROWE. You are still busy in a ROWE. You can still be buried under a mountain of work in a ROWE. But you don't feel overwhelmed. And you don't feel stressed-out and you don't get burned-out.

The reason is that you are in control. When you are in control you have the power to solve problems. This doesn't mean that people aren't supported, that they are on their own, or that they aren't going to work hard. What it means is that people are taking care of business and their lives. They are whole people. Think about that. You are not a different person at work than you are at home. You are taking care of both aspects of your life because it's your life.

So you don't have to feel guilty about neglecting your family when you're at work and guilty about neglecting your work when you're with your family because it's all the same.

Some people get concerned that they will always be working, that taking away those barriers between work and free time means that they will never not be working. It's true that work expands across more hours, but you don't feel overworked in a ROWE because you have that control.

♀ YEAH, BUT . . .

"Stress is good. You need stress to keep people motivated."

We'll give you that—not all stress is bad. We're against the *added* stress of having to account for your time, of having to put on a show of work, and of not having control over your day when things in your life come up and you need to take care of them. At Best Buy, work can be very intense. We would never want to see any person, team, or organization lose their intensity or passion. That's the good stress. The rest, no one needs.

There was a story in the news about French people taking naps at work, and given the way Americans responded you would have thought the French were having sex on their desks. Despite all the studies about how rest increases productivity there was ridicule in the American press. Those nappers are slacking. If they can't handle the workload then someone else can step in and do their jobs. People are whiny and weak.

Maybe it's just that people want to decide when to take a break.

Working hard and feeling stressed and overwhelmed do not make you a hero. It doesn't mean you're tough; it means you're willing to put up with more bullshit than someone else.

Here's an idea that seems radical but isn't in a ROWE: What if you simply don't feel like working today? What if you know that if you go into work today you'll be tired and unmotivated and unfocused and you'd just sleepwalk through your day?

Why go in?
Why waste your time and your company's time?
Why risk making a bad decision?
Why be a distraction to other people who actually want
    to get work done?

In a Results-Only Work Environment, if you're not feeling it that day and you can be reachable by phone and e-mail, and if your work is getting done, then there is no reason you can't simply take the day off.

And this is not a vacation day or sick time or a personal day. You just don't go in. And you don't have to feel guilty.

In a ROWE, all the negative feelings at work are gone. Not just guilt, but also envy. When people get rewarded they get rewarded for achievement, not for playing the game. We can't say it eliminates all politics, but it cuts down on it a lot. People are still going to play favorites but it's harder in a ROWE, because the business goals of an individual or a group become more transparent and more open. People know what other people are trying to accomplish and that is what they are measured on. So if someone gets a promotion they are more likely to deserve it. If something good happens to you then you don't have to feel ashamed about it. Similarly you can't cover up for bad work by playing nice with people. Kissing ass gets you nothing in a ROWE. Isn't that reason enough to make this change?

Every day feels like Saturday.

When we show people this Guidepost they think we are crazy. If every day is a Saturday then people aren't working. They are scamming their employer out of a paycheck. If every day is a Saturday then everyone is at the beach and nothing is getting done.

Of course, we often overestimate how much leisure time we have on Saturdays. For a lot of people we know, Saturdays are very busy because people have to do all the things they weren't allowed to do during the week because their job held them prisoner to time. This is what the forty-hour workweek has done to the weekend. All those demands get pushed to Saturday and Sunday so we can't even enjoy our "free time."

We've talked about how a ROWE spreads work across the week. This Guidepost is about how that *feels*. In a ROWE you are still busy, you are still hardworking, but you do it on your terms. You personalize your time so you get to be productive but you also get to enjoy yourself. Every day you work a little and you play a little and it all blends together.

This is how entrepreneurs and freelancers live. Talk to successful self-employed people and they will describe days that are full but not hectic, that mix personal with professional in a way that is almost seamless. The difference with a ROWE is that you also have the structure of a company. You get to live the life of the self-employed without all the uncertainty and risk. Because that is really the only difference between the entrepreneur and the working man and the regular employee. The entrepreneur can handle the risk and probably even likes the risk. The rest of it—figuring out how to best use your time, being efficient, etc.—all that is stuff that anyone can do. It's not rocket science.

So it's better than Saturday in a way. You get to have your life and also benefit from being part of an organization.

You also get a much greater sense of accomplishment. Work starts to feel more like a personal project. It's like working on your house or your car or doing volunteer work. The task can suck, but you can't beat the feeling of getting things done. A ROWE doesn't take away the struggle of doing your job, but it does give you the sense of accomplishment. You actually feel like you've done something. Because you have. Every day feels like a Saturday because you own every day. Welcome to a life that's yours.

Voices from a ROWE: Beth

Beth is a senior supervisor with a team of thirteen employees. She is in her mid-fifties and has been with Best Buy for five years. She has been in a Results-Only Work Environment for three years.

When we were on the verge of migrating to a Results-Only Work Environment, I remember being anxious. We were sitting in a conference room with other leaders in my area having discussions about ROWE and I actually felt pretty scared about the people on my team and what would happen to our business results. I was really worried that people would get distracted and not keep up with the work. I just couldn't understand how I could let them do whatever they wanted whenever they wanted. How in the world would the work get done?

I was most worried about one particular employee. When I began my position as her manager, she had already been tagged as a low performer: someone who wasn't on top of things, someone you had to watch closely. I'd gotten a lot of negative feedback about her from her previous managers and other team members, and I knew she wouldn't be able to handle this ROWE thing.

I couldn't have been more wrong.

The employee I was worried about has now become my top performer. The year is half over, and she has already done more than she did last year as far as productivity goes. And she's working out-of-state. Pre-ROWE, if she had told me she was moving out of the state, I never would have even entertained the thought. Now that she's flourishing in a ROWE, I would do anything to keep her. She's outperforming every standard we had before, so I don't care where she is! I truly believe that giving her ownership of how she spends her time has done wonders. I can only wonder how many other "low performers" out there have the same potential. If just given the freedom to control their time, they might soar just like my "low performer" has.

Looking at my entire team, I am in awe of what ROWE has done for our productivity. I am setting extremely high goals for them and they're reaching them with no problems. And no complaining. If I had set these types of goals pre-ROWE, they would have kicked and screamed and gone to HR to complain.

Whenever we reach our goals, we always set the next set of goals a little higher. Here's what's happening: A good year for us pre-ROWE used to be completing 300 audits in a year. Last year, in a ROWE, we completed 612 audits—*double* what good used to look like. This year we're on track to exceed last year. And we've lost one team member, so we're doing it with fewer people than we had pre-ROWE.

Part of this productivity gain is because ROWE has changed our team dynamic. Everyone wants to help one another now. When someone is finished with their own audits, they ask their coworkers if they can help them with theirs. It's no longer "This is my work and that's your work." It's now *our* work. At another company, they might try to do team-building event after team-building event to try to get this kind of teamwork happening, but we've done none of that. It's just something that ROWE creates naturally.

Aside from the productivity gain, the best thing for me as a manager in a ROWE is not having to be the hall monitor. I used to hear things all the time from my employees like "So-and-so took a twenty-minute smoke break" or "So-and-so was playing games on the Internet." Now no one cares. Pre-ROWE, I heard this kind of nonsense every time I would come back from a meeting. That kind of stuff is such a waste of every-one's time. That backbiting and gossip is so typical in a work environment. In a ROWE, I don't have to deal with it any-more.

My employees don't have to make up excuses to be sick anymore. I just had an employee who had to stay home to get her water meter changed. Pre-ROWE, she would have made up an excuse to be home and would have turned in some kind of time-off notice. Imagine a forty-year-old having to make up an excuse like that! Don't you think it's demeaning to make adults lie? Think of how many hours of productivity we lose from people because they call in sick for things like this when they could be working. It's crazy.

The hardest thing for me as a manager about migrating to a ROWE was giving up control. I thought I had control over my people before. I thought if I could see them all in their cubes that they were working hard for me. Now that I'm in a ROWE, I realize that was all just an illusion—I really had no idea what they were doing. As managers, we're bound to this illusion. It's time to let go and really see what our employees can do.

CHAPTER SEVEN

What's Next for ROWE

By the time this book is published almost everyone at Best Buy corporate will be in a ROWE, but there is still a lot of work to do. For starters, we need to make sure that Best Buy's success with ROWE doesn't erode. While people who are in a ROWE would do anything to keep their new situation, individual teams or departments can still backslide. First, all of those early adopters are going to need a ROWE refresher. Second, even those who are successfully living in a ROWE need support. Until other companies get on board with ROWE, there is a chance that the rest of the world will view Best Buy as a curiosity (and Sludge it). There are also still people within the company who would rather see the old ways return. Which would suck.

Fortunately, we have some factors working to our advantage, such as tangible results. In the middle stages of rolling out ROWE at Best Buy, the sociologists Phyllis Moen and Erin Kelly from the University of Minnesota's Flexible Work and Well-Being Center came on-site to study the effects of a Results-Only Work Environment on employees. Their study, which was funded by the National Institutes of Health, was a rare opportunity to watch an organic, natural experiment with a nontraditional way of working.

As part of their study, Moen and Kelly kept track of 658 employees. Half went from being in a traditional work environment to starting their life in a ROWE; half continued in a traditional work environment. They compared the experiences of these employees before ROWE and six months later, after half had migrated. Using surveys, they targeted four areas of concern: control over work time, overall health, work behaviors, and organizational commitment. Because it typically takes a year for migration to take place, their findings are geared toward the beginning of the change process, but even so they found dramatic results across age, gender, and employment level. (For a link to the complete study, please visit www.culturerx.com.)

The good news was the people did not report an increase in work hours. Some people worry that because a Results-Only Work Environment ignores time as a measure, either employees would feel more pressure to work longer hours, or employers would try to squeeze more time out of people. But that wasn't the case. What did change was that people felt a big increase in work-schedule fit. Forty-two percent (compared to 23 percent in the control group) said they felt their work schedule fit their life better, while 53 percent said they had more time to take care of all aspects of their life (compared with 39 percent for the control). One quarter of people had an increase in sleep and 41 percent felt an increase in energy compared with 35 percent of the control group. On the job people felt less pressure to work overtime and do unnecessary work. The

ROWE group also said they experienced fewer work interruptions. Perhaps one of the most striking changes was in what the researchers call "turnover intention" which, in lay terms, is the desire to leave. A full third of the people in a ROWE were happier to stay than in the control group.

A number of the psychological and health indicators such as overall well-being, emotional exhaustion, and psychological distress didn't change in the study. We have qualitative stories to demonstrate that change, but the study's numbers weren't there . . . yet. We say yet because the bigger changes in people's personal lives seem to happen in a ROWE over time.

Even so, the results from this study are unusual by most measures. Most current studies in "work redesign" have investigated cases in which companies have increased employee access to flextime policies or other top-down solutions. So far the results have been undramatic, which is not surprising given that most approaches to work-life balance issues involve technical change and not social change.

We're still waiting for the study that looks at the long-term effects of ROWE, but anecdotally we have evidence that it makes substantial changes in people's lives. Javier's story about taking care of his mom during a family crisis is not atypical. Scores of employees have extraordinary stories about how a ROWE has allowed them to go back to graduate school, take care of sick loved ones, or spend time with relatives in other countries. We've also heard everyday, but equally encouraging, stories about people spending more time with their kids, their spouses, even their dogs. When we say that a ROWE gives people their life back, we really mean it.

Giving people control over their time isn't a magic bullet.

People aren't automatically going to become trim and fit and stress-free (although one person did note that their skin cleared up after their team migrated into a ROWE). People will still have to improve their own lives. But at least a ROWE gives them that chance.

ROWE also gives businesses a chance to thrive and grow in surprising ways too. We almost hate to do this, because we're not graph-and-table-type people, but sometimes a nice bar graph makes it all clear:

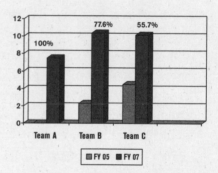

Voluntary Turnover Rates

In ROWE teams, Voluntary Turnover Rates are trending down.

The company is RETAINING Talent.

Involuntary Turnover Rates

In ROWE teams, Involuntary Turnover Rates are trending up.

Managers are focused on PERFORMANCE.

The chart tells us that ROWE teams at Best Buy are experiencing a decrease in voluntary turnover rate, meaning the company is retaining the talent. ROWE teams also experience an increase in involuntary turnover rates indicating that unsatisfactory performers are exposed. Furthermore—and we swear this is the last time we'll do this—the financial gains are very real:

Cost Savings Associated with Reduction in Voluntary Turnover

ROWE Team	Number of Employees	Voluntary Turnover FY05	Voluntary Turnover FY07	Voluntary Turnover Improvement	Average Turnover Cost per Employee	Voluntary Turnover Savings
Team A	~140	15.51%	0.00%	15.51%	$102,000.00	$2,214,828.00
Team B	~187	18.50%	2.31%	16.19%	$102,000.00	$3,088,080.60
Team C	~50	31.46%	4.49%	26.97%	$102,000.00	$1,375,470.00

In a Results-Only Work Environment, productivity is measured by "perceived gain." The CultureRx Post-Migration Culture Audit uses a sliding scale of 1–100 percent. Managers and employees report individual perceptions of their productivity gain by choosing a point on the sliding scale. If an employee reports a perceived productivity gain of, say, 40 percent, and the manager (who is measuring "business outcomes") reports a gain in the outcome of projected business targets, then the perceived productivity is actually driving real results.

For example, the CultureRx Post Culture Audit reported an average 44.59 percent perceived gain in productivity for Team C. During the time that the perceived gain was measured, Team C realized a more than 50 percent increase in cost reductions year-over-year without adding additional employees. With other variables staying the same, management in this area says that operating in a ROWE has definitely contributed to their success.

These kinds of results are also happening with people at Best Buy who are doing production work. In Team A, department management is reporting a 10 to 20 percent increase in productivity per employee, which has resulted in an approximate $10 million annual benefit for the company.

This is not to say that there aren't additional challenges to ROWE. For example, right now there are people at Best Buy who are trying to figure out how to handle vacation policy from an accounting perspective. In terms of productivity, it's good that people aren't taking time off like they used to for doctor appointments or family emergencies or burnout—they're just working through the obstacles. But keep in mind that for companies, vacation time is a liability—it must be paid off when an employee leaves, so it's carried as debt. With exempt employees not taking vacation hours off, the company's vacation banks are going up.

Once this change moves beyond Best Buy, we envision human resources policies across corporate America coming under question. Mealtimes, break times, sick leave, bereavement policies—any tool we currently use to deal with employees as people starts to look strange in a ROWE, where people get to be people all the time. A ROWE can turn a business's world upside down. But mostly it's the bad stuff that gets turned upside down. The good aspects of work—that people want to make an impact, that they want to grow personally and professionally, that they want to make money and be passionate about what they do—none of that changes.

If we've done our job right then you are now asking yourself what you can do to bring ROWE into your life. This is indeed the next challenge: How do you take something that grew and evolved organically within an organization over the course of several years and share it with the rest of the world? How do you advance the cause of ROWE?

We don't use the word *cause* lightly. As much as a ROWE is a new way of working it is just as easily described as a new way of living. We want to see the entire world in a ROWE, from the most powerful executive to the entry-level "peon" who is so new to the company they don't know where the bathrooms are yet. In order to do this we're going to need to educate people about ROWE, to advocate that individuals and companies change, and to advocate for our rights under this new way of thinking. For more information on what we're doing to lead this movement visit www.culturerx.com. But in the meantime we offer these words of advice.

First, we're asking that people who are excited about this idea explore their own attitudes and beliefs about work. At the end of this book we have included a "How ROWE Are You?" quiz. We encourage you to take the quiz yourself and give it to your friends. There is a score at the end, but that's less important than going through the exercise of figuring out how your own particular workplace ticks. The quiz is a good way of opening your eyes to the gritty details of why work sucks for *you*.

The next thing you can do is start working on your own behavior. Think back to the littering example in chapter three. Once people realized that they were polluting their highways, cities, and neighborhoods, they changed. You stop throwing that soda can out the window of your car. Just taking that step means something when you're tackling a problem that requires social change.

It's the same with Sludge. Practice not Sludging people. At first you're still going to think Sludge, but if you can avoid saying it that is going to make a difference. Refuse (quietly or noisily) to take part in Sludge Conspiracies. Reassure people who are Sludge Justifying that you don't need to hear their time excuse, and work on not Sludge Justifying yourself. If they're getting their work done, you have no beef with them. And watch yourself when you find yourself Sludge Anticipating. All that worry is a waste of energy and brain power.

Once you're not Sludging, you will find a change comes over some people—not all, but some. When you stop justifying your actions in the face of time, you'll find that some people will stop slinging Sludge. Whether they consciously realize it or not, it's no fun for them to fling crap if they're not getting a reaction out of you. The same goes for Sludge Conspiracies. If you don't participate, if you don't show yourself to be part of the tribe, then people won't include you in their nonsense. People who want to engage in Back Sludge have to go elsewhere to get their Sludge fix.

We also encourage people to start using terms like Sludge. We've found that a powerful way to face adversity is to name it. Now that we have a name for it, use it. You can say to people, calmly, nonaccusingly, "That's Sludge." Not only will you call them on it, you just might start an interesting and necessary conversation about the attitudes behind that comment. Even little changes in your language can have big effects. When talking about these work-life balance issues, stop using the word flexibility and start using the word control ("I'm looking for a job with control" as opposed to "I'm looking for a job with flexibility"). Stop using the words *early* and *late* and antiquated terms like *by the end of business today*. Stop talking about how many hours you work or how hard you're working. But by all means start using the word *results*.

Whether you're talking to your coworker or manager or even your friends and family, steer those conversations toward what really needs to get done. What are the results we're trying to drive?

We think you'll find that taking even small actions along these lines will not only make work suck a little less, but you'll also find that conversations will naturally steer toward the concept of ROWE. Which brings us to the final thing you can do to advance this cause, and that's spread the word.

In addition to helping the approximately three thousand people at Best Buy corporate headquarters migrate into a ROWE, for the past two years we have been traveling around the country speaking to business leaders, community organizations, schools, law firms, health care organizations, and anyone else who is willing to listen. As a result we've gotten pretty comfortable with the storm of Yeah, Buts that kick up every time we talk about these ideas. And we can see how an individual who is new to this idea might balk at trying to talk to other people about ROWE. Where to begin? How to handle all those Yeah, Buts? Do I focus on the human results or the business results? How do I explain Sludge, or our concepts like time, belief, and judgment?

First of all, a word about integrity. In our minds ROWE is a movement that will live or die on people being able to teach, inspire, and lead, not trick, bully, or intimidate. That's the old model, the top-down model that management has used to scare you or trick you into thinking that worthless time-management seminar is really going to change your life. You can't force people into a ROWE; you have to inspire people to believe in this change. So we're not asking people to push ROWE onto the world. We're looking for believers who want other people to believe because it's right.

Second, all those Yeah, Buts come from the same place: belief. People raise objections to the logistics of a ROWE because as much as they think work sucks, they believe it's the only way to go. Most people have not thought deep and long about why and how the workplace should function. We inherit these attitudes and all those Yeah, Buts are just the sound of someone getting riled up by your challenging their beliefs.

Finally, we encourage you to have fun when talking about ROWE. We once read an article about how the majority of the jokes in *The Simpsons* are about religion, and we can see why: People's beliefs are funny. We're not advocating that you belittle or ridicule people (or at least not too much) but those daily reminders of the absurdity of work are all around us. One of our favorites is when we're on an airplane after a short flight and as soon as the plane lands people whip out their cell phones and call in to the office to tell someone that they've landed. Then they go through this elaborate ritual of checking to make sure no one needed them (even though if someone did they'd probably have left a voice mail) and then to give the play-by-play of how they're going to taxi to the gate, then go through baggage claim, then rent a car, then go to the hotel, etc. And we imagine the poor person on the other end of the line sagging into their chair having to listen when not only do they not care, but *it doesn't matter where the caller is.* The only reason the caller is checking in is that they believe in availability. So in other words, funny.

Still, there are some tactics you can use that we have found effective in introducing a ROWE to someone who has never heard of the idea. And so, in the hope that you'll go forth and multiply, here is the

Cocktail Party–Backyard BBQ–Watercooler–Bus Stop–Family Reunion Guide to Talking About a ROWE

1. Talk about how work sucks.

Whenever we talk about a ROWE we keep ideas like the 13 Guideposts for later in the presentation. If people aren't ready for ideas like every meeting being optional, or that you can go see a movie on a Thursday afternoon, they can shut down. So we start by talking about how work sucks.

Your goal here is to listen and to guide, not to lecture. The trick is to let the person you're talking to discover the one thing for them that really ticks them off about work. It might be their company's break policy. It might be the fact that they get Sludge for being late because they have a long commute and it's hard to get in "on time." It could be anything and everyone is different, but everyone also has something about work that angers them, that they connect with on a very emotional, visceral level. If you get them beyond the kind of run-of-the-mill bitching that we all engage in, you're that much closer. If they're riled up about work, then they might be ready for a new perspective.

2. Wonder about an alternative.

When we do our presentations we ask people to imagine their ideal state of work. What would a day look like if you didn't have to fill hours? What would work look like if there was no such thing as being late? What if you got paid for a chunk of work and not a chunk of time?

Again your job here is not to lecture but to allow that person to discover what they already intuitively know: Measuring work based on time and physical presence is stupid.

> Isn't it funny that we reward people for putting in long hours when we don't know for a fact that those long hours are amounting to anything?
> Isn't it funny that we rush to work every day and then spend the first hour at our desk reading the paper and drinking coffee?
> Isn't it funny that if you're done with your work for the day at four, you can't just leave? Why do you have to stay that extra hour and pretend to be busy?

3. Introduce ROWE.

What you want to get across at this point is that in a Results-Only Work Environment time is no longer a factor in judging performance. People get paid for a chunk of work, not for a chunk of time. Also, focus on the results. People have to do their job to keep their job. ROWE is like college. Work hard and study hard and you'll get good grades. Party and slack off and you won't.

Whenever we get too far offtrack in our meetings with people we always bring it back to this simple idea. Currently we are rewarding people for a mixture of time plus results. In today's global, 24/7 economy this doesn't make sense. Let's reward people for work, not time.

4. Watch for the fork.

When we stand in front of audiences and talk about ROWE, there is an immediate polarizing effect. The idea that in a Results-Only Work Environment people can do whatever they want, whenever they want, as long as the work gets done creates strong reactions, both positive and negative. Even the idea, talked about in the abstract, of a Results-Only Work Environment is like a personality test. The gut reaction is either strongly for or strongly against, and part of your job is to pay attention to who gets it right away and who is resistant. Watch for that split and then move on to step five.

5. Work on the people who get it and don't worry so much about the ones who don't.

One manager was so upset by the philosophy of ROWE that they said ROWE would "bring down the company" and "make it impossible for us to become a global business." In cases like this when you're speaking to a group you can remain silent and let others chime in with their thoughts. Usually other people see how ROWE actually does the opposite. If you're with only one person, smile and walk away—directly to the bar to freshen your drink. Then go off and talk to someone else.

Even to the sympathetic listener you can acknowledge that a ROWE sounds crazy, but then quickly follow up that acknowledgment by noting two things. First, a Results-Only Work Environment is already working. This isn't a theory or a wish. The corporate headquarters of a Fortune 100 company has embraced this idea and it's working for them both financially and in terms of employee happiness.

Second, you can always remind people why there is a need for a ROWE in the first place. Keep in mind that all those initial objections about a ROWE are based on people's beliefs about how work gets done and what work looks like. Those objections are tied to the clock and our ideas about time. But everyone knows work sucks, and if you've done the early steps right, then they've already admitted it.

6. Encourage them to learn more and support their efforts to understand.

People have been burned so many times by fake change that they might need some proof that this is real. You can admit that everyone has seen a lot of teach-and-train programs come and go. They might want to know what makes a ROWE different. That's a good question and you don't have to shy away from it. Because this is real change it takes work. People have to create and customize the ROWE that works for them.

This is going to sound like a cliché, like therapy-speak, but people really do have to let go. Whatever language you use, whether it's coming to terms with change, or letting go, or making your peace, or whatever you want to call it, that's what people have to do: Let go of the old way of working and commit themselves to the new way of working. It might take work, but it's worth it.

And you might find unlikely allies in unlikely places. You can't assume that someone who is objecting isn't on your side. When the University of Minnesota researchers came to give their results to a group of people at Best Buy there was one guy asking really hard questions. If you didn't know him and understand his personality you might think he hated ROWE and showed up at that meeting to shoot us down. In reality he is one of ROWE's biggest supporters. He was asking the hard questions—he was really grilling us and the researchers—because he wants it to succeed. He knows that some people will need little convincing, but that some people will need overwhelming evidence that it works. So he was extra critical. He knew that it wasn't an easy fight and so he was arming himself with the tools he needed to make ROWE work in his group.

A final thought on talking to people about ROWE: Stay calm. We're not going to win this by arguing. So find that one thing about ROWE that you find unshakably true. For some people it's the fact that you always come back to results. For others it's the idea that everyone has a right to be treated like an adult. Or for others it's the fact that people have a right to their time. Whatever it is, remember that one true thing and use it as a fallback. As much as people try to fight you on this, you always have that core belief that will keep you going.

And remember the bottom line to end all bottom lines. Remind your listener that in a ROWE you get rewarded with control over your time. Ask them to imagine how powerful an incentive that is. To be trusted to do your job. To be treated like an adult. Isn't that worth almost anything? If you could be given that kind of control and freedom, then wouldn't you work your ass off to deliver results? Because that's what happens. Once people have a taste of what a ROWE offers they never want to work any other way.

We think of ROWE as a people's movement. That's how it started, not as an edict from on high. Not as a new management tool. But ROWE couldn't have thrived without some fearless and supportive leaders at the top of the organization.

Also, contrary to how they are seen in business culture, managers and directors are people too. They deserve the benefits of a ROWE just as much as the rank and file do.

As Beth's story illustrates, for managers and directors the journey into a ROWE is just as transformative as it is for the rank-and-file employee. But because bosses have power, their experience is a little different.

For starters, most managers realize how poorly they were treating people. Even if they were a "good boss" they were still guilty of Sludge. We've heard managers confess that they didn't realize what kind of pain and heartache they were causing their people, even with what they saw as innocent comments. They don't know that even a little dig like "nice of you to join us" could really hurt not only someone's health and well-being, but also their loyalty, engagement, and productivity. So the first thing managers experience is something akin to grief. They thought they were doing their job. They thought they were even helping people. But then managers realize that they have been parenting adults. And they feel terrible.

As managers migrate into a ROWE the next step usually involves a certain amount of fear. They get scared when they realize they haven't been abundantly clear to people about what they are supposed to be doing. Now that they are in a ROWE the only thing they have to focus on is results. Before they were protected by title and power, but now any flaws in their management style are exposed. So they have to stop hiding and really figure out what their employees are supposed to be doing and how that connects to the bigger goals of the organization.

But once they start to figure out how to go from parent to mentor, from boss to leader, they emerge with a richer relationship with their people. They have a more human relationship with their employees and their work relationship is stronger too. That focus on results can really work wonders on communication, planning, and execution.

We've even seen people who came out of a military background change their thinking. People who were literally schooled in the command-and-control model realize that it wasn't good for their employees, it wasn't good for business, and it wasn't good for them. We've also seen chronic management-by-walking-around types stop walking around and trust their employees to do their jobs. People used to cringe when they saw these kinds of bosses because they knew they were in for an unnecessary interruption. Now those bosses are appreciated.

We know from experience that a lot of managers already practice an under-the-radar, modified ROWE. We now challenge those leaders to take it a step further. Or maybe you've undergone a management conversion while reading this book. Maybe you realize you've been a bit of a control freak and you'd like to change. If you're a manager and this sounds good to you, then there are a handful of tips we can give so you can start exploring a ROWE with your team.

How to Focus on Results with Your Team

Stop relying on human resources to do the "people" part of your job—get clear about performance goals, communicate often, and hold people accountable.

You lose your credibility when you bring in HR to have the tough conversations. When your employees aren't performing, *talk* to them. Find out why and rather than focus on how hard they're working or the amount of hours they're putting in, focus on the work itself. What do they need to do to succeed?

Break time? Lunchtime? Attendance policy? Absence pay? Personal time? Tardiness policy? Look at the policies and rules and throw out the ones that are stupid!

Many policies were written decades ago and haven't changed —and companies copy one another's policies because that's what work is. Many policies are not government-regulated policies—they're internal rules that make children out of adults. We need to get real about the employee manual. It's culture that makes the place go, not rules in a book nobody reads except the people in HR.

Reward employees based on results, not on how much "time" they put in at the office.

Instead of saying, "James put in a lot of extra hours this month—good for James!" talk about what James actually contributed. What did he do for the company? Do not use any reference to time. Otherwise, your team will compete to "out-time" everyone else to get attention.

Don't prescribe what work-life balance looks like for your employees.

"Well, you have a kid, so you'll need to make sure they're in day care when you're home working, otherwise you won't get anything done."

"Wow, it's six-thirty—you should really go home now and spend time with your family."

It's not up to you. It's up to them.

Don't handpick who gets to be flexible and who doesn't.

Okay?

Don't think that you're a great boss if during a snowstorm you "let" your people "leave early."

Sending out an e-mail "letting" people take time off for a project well-done, or a snowstorm—or whatever—is another way to make people feel like children. It reinforces the fact that you have control over their time and they don't. Let people make this decision themselves.

Stop managing by walking around.

Every time you "check in" on someone they have to stop what they were doing, reorient their thinking from doing the work to give you a spontaneous presentation about the job they are doing, and then, once you leave, reorient themselves back to doing the work. Either send them an e-mail, or better yet, plan.

Trust your people like you trust yourself.

Stop making rules for the few you're afraid won't live up to your expectations. Or rules that protect you from the incompetence of the few but hinder the performance of the many. Your goal is to make work as unlike grade school as possible.

Voices from a ROWE: Charlotte

*Charlotte is an individual contributor in the dot-com division.
She is in her early thirties and has been in a ROWE for three
years.*

My son says, "ROWE is about riding bikes, getting pets, playing games, and having fun." This means the world to me because my relationship with my son has changed so much since
ROWE.

Before ROWE I would get up, get my son dressed, drop
him off at school, and not arrive at work until nine. Whenever
I took a new position, I always had to have sit-down conversations with my managers to let them know that I wouldn't be
able to make it into the office until nine. because I had to drop
my son at school. Those conversations felt terrible—I always
felt like I was playing "Captain May I?" and asking for favors.
Inevitably, there would be meetings that would come up at
eight or eight thirty and I would try to find someone to watch
my son, but sometimes I couldn't. Then, of course, I'd feel like
I wasn't being a team player.

I didn't have any way of getting my work done outside the

hours of nine and five, so absolutely everything had to be done within those hours in the office. I usually ate lunch at my desk. I didn't take many breaks—I just plowed through my work day in and day out.

When I was still living in the "old world" I didn't feel like I was making as much headway in my career because my co-workers could work longer hours. I would try to be as outspoken as I could, but I'm not good at tooting my own horn, or "managing up" as people call it. When you're not good at that, it takes a lot of energy to promote yourself and it can cause a huge amount of stress.

When I first migrated to a Results-Only Work Environment, I wanted people to know I was still getting my work done. I would send e-mails at six thirty in the evening or on Friday nights to let people know I was working. I made sure to do these kinds of things especially on days I had left early. Then I just let go of all that. I started focusing on my work, actually the great work I was doing for the company. My stress level is much different now. It's shifted to the results I need to achieve.

Now I can't *not* be involved in my son's life or his school, when before it just wasn't ever an option for me. I used to have to deplete all my vacation and personal time to help my son with his school activities. Now I just go to them and I don't feel guilty. I've been able to get to know his teachers.

I get my son ready for his soccer games now without being in a rush. We can actually sit down and have something to eat beforehand instead of rushing to the games on empty stomachs. During the summer, I'm able to be with my son instead of putting him in a summer program five days a week. This Friday we're going to the Minnesota State Fair. He plays with his friends outside while I work on my laptop. I feel like I'm giving him more of a childhood now.

Fun and spontaneous stuff doesn't always and shouldn't always come on the weekend. And I want my son to know that too. A few weeks back, after I attended a couple of meetings, I picked him up from his grandmother's house around noon, fully prepared to go get ice cream and go back to our house and do work for a couple of hours more that afternoon. Well, he had other ideas. He talked me into renting a kayak and spending the afternoon on the lake instead. Then I just logged on to work later in the evening. So what is he going to remember? And what values do I want him to learn?

One of the biggest moments for me since I migrated to a ROWE was when my son told me he wanted to be a mom when he grew up. He watches the way I'm able to be part of his life now and knows that's a possibility for him when he gets older too. I think it's so cool how he sees me, his mom, as someone he wants to model himself after. His friends see me coming into school to be with him during his activities, they know I work for Best Buy, and they think this company is the best.

CHAPTER EIGHT

ROWE Update: Beyond Best Buy

Why Work Sucks and How to Fix It was first published in May 2008, which, looking back, seems like a different world. The first dominoes in the subprime mortgage mess were falling, but the financial collapse hadn't hit in full. The business leaders we talked to were still confident and optimistic. Their worries had less to do with protecting themselves from disaster and more to do with maximizing success and finding competitive advantages.

But it wasn't long before we found ourselves evangelizing for ROWE in a completely different economic climate than the one in which it had developed. In some ways you couldn't pick a worse time to introduce to the world a new way of working. In addition to massive layoffs, businesses were cutting training and development budgets. They were eliminating or severely curbing traditional flexible work arrangements. Compounding the problem was an aura of almost crippling fear. We had binged on too much risk and now it was time to turtle up and get back to basics. Not exactly the best time for innovation and change.

At the same time, as we launched our consulting business

we not only found a willing audience for a Results-Only Work Environment, but a population of early adopters who were instantly galvanized by this idea. We achieved a formal separation from Best Buy and went out into the world looking for the next generation of ROWE warriors. We hit the lecture circuit and started working with new companies eager to make this change.

What we found was that despite economic uncertainty—and in some cases because of it—there were people who saw ROWE as an opportunity to increase engagement and productivity, to retain talent, and to confront the new normal by looking past the haze created by the traditional work environment and having genuine conversations about the direction and purpose of their businesses.

When we wrote this book, we set out to make it a manifesto. The idea of putting forth the typical argument-and-evidence approach of business books was too sober, too middle ground. We wanted this book to grab people by the lapels and shake them awake, and it did. What made this book so exciting for many people was that it took what entrepreneurial business leaders were already doing and brought it to the logical extreme. ROWE gave them a language and a framework for moving from results-*oriented* to results-*only*. Now they had both the permission and the tools to neutralize those lingering attitudes and beliefs from the traditional work environment and take the next step forward.

One great early adopter success story is that of the Girl Scouts of San Gorgonio Council, a midsize nonprofit organization that serves fifteen thousand girls and five thousand adult volunteers in Riverside and San Bernardino counties in southern California just outside Los Angeles. In the spring of

2008, right before this book came out, new CEO Jessica Lawrence was struggling with what she saw as the disconnect between the Girl Scouts's mission and the way her organization traditionally was run.

"Before becoming CEO, I had been COO and director of development, so I'd experienced life as a staff member in an organization where the clock ruled and the hierarchy ruled," says Lawrence. "I really didn't like the way these antiquated policies and procedures made me feel, but I also felt that we were dishonoring the mission of the organization. We're trying to empower girls to feel like they can grow up to be anything they can dream of being, but then we had an organization that was unfriendly to working mothers and to anyone who had any kind of life outside work. I felt that if we were going to advocate for girls to reach their full potential, then we also needed to take the lead in creating the kind of workplaces that would allow them to flourish."

In June 2008 she happened to pick up a copy of *Why Work Sucks and How to Fix It* at an airport bookstore. When her plane landed she got on the phone with her HR director, Daniel Malyszka, urging him to read the book immediately so they could talk about how to implement ROWE.

"There was so much in the book that aligned with what I had been thinking," she says. "In addition to wanting to change our culture for higher level reasons, I also had concerns about how we were serving our customers. Most of our volunteers are parents, and it didn't make sense for them to only be able to contact us during traditional business hours. The book's message about trusting people also hit home. We were in the process of piloting a telework program in response to rising gas prices, but we had limited the program to only certain levels of employees. One of our hourly employees had come to me and asked why it was that the people who were paid the most had the option to work at home and save money when the people who made the least didn't have that option. You get paid more so you're trusted more? There was something wrong with that."

The next step was to gather senior leadership and management to spend a day going through the Guideposts. Lawrence and her staff talked through the challenges of this new way of working, with special attention paid to how the managers would adapt.

"With ROWE there is a huge emphasis on managers managing differently," she says. "The ROWE experience is in some ways defined by how a manager modifies his or her style. The idea that every meeting is optional was hard for some people, especially those who wielded meetings like a sword as a way of exerting control over their staff."

But the managers quickly got onboard, and by the middle of July they were ready to roll it out to the staff. Lawrence and her management team developed their own "Hello ROWE!" presentation. Some of the staff members performed Sludge skits, and time was spent going over the 13 Guideposts and what they did and didn't mean. Then, right that afternoon, Lawrence announced that from that moment forward everyone was free to do whatever they wanted whenever they wanted as long as the work got done.

"I thought it was important for everyone to feel unleashed," Lawrence says. "I wanted them to know that they were trusted. That they didn't have to feel like protecting themselves."

Policy changes, goal writing, and other more day-to-day aspects of ROWE came later. First people had to learn that they didn't have to check in with every decision, that they didn't have to funnel ideas up the chain of command. Lawrence also got rid of the permission slips (you had to *apply* to be out of the office for more than an hour for a doctor's appointment) and sign-in sheets and request forms.

"It helped them see how productive they could be on their own," she says. "In the end I think this led to them writing more challenging results for themselves when we did get to that stage of the process. Once they started working in a ROWE they realized they were more creative, that they were able to give more of their best selves. They realized they had more to give, and so the goals they set for themselves were more ambitious than they would have been if we'd made them write goals before we went live."

By October 1, 2008, the staff had had enough success with ROWE that the board of directors officially supported the change in policy. Since then, Girl Scouts of San Gorgonio Council has experienced outstanding results from the change. In confidential surveys taken after the migration, employees reported an increase of good or great "control of time" from 29 percent pre-ROWE to 100 percent post-ROWE. The percent of employees reporting good or great "work-life balance" increased from 18 percent pre-ROWE to 93 percent post-ROWE. The percent of employees reporting good or great "focus when working," "productivity when working," and "efficiency when working" increased from about half pre-ROWE to almost 100 percent post-ROWE. Lawrence says that sustaining ROWE has come naturally because the culture change is complete. The rigid formality of their workplace is gone, replaced by freer, easier, and more frequent communication.

The outside world has taken notice, too. In 2010, the *Nonprofit Times* voted Girl Scouts of San Gorgonio the third best nonprofit to work for of organizations their size. Overall they ranked eighth. In addition, thanks to ROWE, Girl Scouts of San Gorgonio Council has had a significant drop in voluntary turnover, from 16.25 percent to 9.75 percent, which is a noteworthy sign of their new ability to retain employees. "People are always tempted by bigger money," says Lawrence. "But we've had employees tell us that because of ROWE they'd have to be paid $25,000 more to consider leaving, and even that may not be enough. For a nonprofit looking to stay competitive this is especially important. Many of our recent hires are people from the for-profit world who are looking for more balance. ROWE gives me an incredible hiring advantage, and it's kind of mind-boggling to me that more people haven't jumped onboard."

Gap Finds an Edge Over the Competition

Eric Severson, vice president of HR for Gap Inc. Outlet, a division of Gap Inc., was also drawn to the business benefits of ROWE. Gap Inc. Outlet operates over three hundred Gap Outlet and Banana Republic Factory stores. The division employs fourteen thousand total, but even though the three hundred headquarters workers only represent a fraction of the whole, their contribution is disproportionately significant. "We're a private label business," says Severson. "Everything we sell is designed, sourced, and managed at headquarters. If the product isn't compelling, then we don't make our numbers."

Severson, who led the charge at Gap to implement ROWE, says that the early- to mid-2000s were a particularly challenging time for his headquarters HR team, which manages the people who develop the products. The labor market was on fire, which made it harder to attract and retain talent. Compounding the problem was Gap's location. San Francisco's cost of living is among the highest in the country (with one of the scarcest housing markets) and is consistently ranked one of the top five cities with the worst commute. The Bay Area is also home to talent competitors like Williams-Sonoma, Levi's, Gymboree, and Restoration Hardware.

"Our competitive advantage in the talent market has always been that our employees at all levels find their work fun, interesting, and challenging—but there was too much of a good thing," says Severson. "People were living at the office. During exit interviews, we heard the same refrain: 'I love my job, but it's just not worth it anymore.'"

Retention became a huge issue. At one point turnover rates for key functions such as merchandising and planning were as high as 38 percent in the Outlet division. The fact that 74 percent of the workforce was female and skewing Gen Y meant that the lack of work-life balance affected Gap to a greater extent than it did its competitors. For Severson and his team the opportunity wasn't just to turn the work culture around, but also to create a competitive advantage.

In 2005, they dabbled in technical change. There was a Laptops for All initiative, a no-meetings Fridays policy, and other efforts to cut down on nonessential work. Then Severson went to the Conference Board's Work Life Conference, where he saw us speak. "That's the answer," he remembers thinking. "It gets at the problem at its root instead of just treating symptoms."

At the time, Severson says, the company wasn't quite ready for such a seemingly radical shift, but then in 2008 a change in

the retail industry provided the catalyst. Along with other re-
tailers, Gap Inc. Outlet started e-sourcing, which involves
conducting live, online auctions with overseas vendors. Their
production people would be up in the middle of the night
managing bids from vendors in China, for example, but then
they were expected to be back in the office at 8:15 A.M. in order
to be "on time."

"It didn't make sense and it wasn't sustainable," Severson
says.

In the spring of 2008, Severson and the vice president of
production, Sonia Syngal, conducted a "quiet" ROWE pilot
with the production team. Then, in the fall, with the support
of the division president, Art Peck, the pilot was expanded to
137 Outlet employees across all product functions. Severson
and his HR team were also careful to make sure they measured *everything*.

"It was very important that we *not* do what most people
do with these kinds of initiatives," says Severson, "which is
to launch a program and then ask 'How did you like it?' after
it's over."

Before the program started, Severson's team conducted
surveys with members of the pilot groups, with internal and
external customers, as well as with the managers of migrating
teams in areas such as productivity, accountability, efficiency,
and engagement. Then members of the product and store support group (production, visual merchandising, merchandising
and inventory management, communications, etc.) went
through the process.

"The first metric was that we do no harm," says Severson.
"And not a single score went down. In fact, the results were
remarkable."

Turnover for the initial production pilot group dropped by 50 percent, while engagement scores went up 13 percentage points, the best performance in the division. The pilot group's internal and external customers agreed. Gap Inc. Sourcing (the people involved in those pesky online auctions) reported a 72 percent increase in efficiency and a 45 percent improvement in responsiveness, and found the group had achieved a record 85 percent in its high degree of accountability. The follow-up cross-functional pilot produced similar results.

Once the pilot was a success, Severson and the executive leadership team of Outlet started lobbying to take ROWE divisionwide.

"We had to get approval every step of the way, so we showed our senior executives irrefutable ROI statistics," says Severson.

The full migration for the entire Outlet division was approved in June 2009. There was another round of pre- and postsurveying. In February 2010, the company's leadership was satisfied that ROWE was working and granted it status as a "steady state" program.

In the meantime, the economy had radically changed. Turnover rates would likely have dropped anyway, but ROWE continues to deliver beyond industry norms. Gap Inc. Outlet had a 7 percent headquarters turnover rate in 2008 and 2009, which was lower than that found in other divisions. Furthermore, word has gotten out into the San Francisco job market. Outside job candidates have started asking about ROWE, and people within Outlet are turning down promotions in other divisions and jobs at other companies because they don't want to lose the benefits of this change. Meanwhile, engagement scores remain very high, with Outlet employees averaging

88 percent in 2009 (compared to the national average of 43 percent).

"In all my years in HR I've never encountered a single talent management program that delivered such a high return on such a low investment," says Severson. "Personally, I consider the advantage in the marketplace we've achieved with ROWE to be the biggest triumph of my career. We made a difference in the bottom line—and that's the goal of every business leader."

"The main reason we pushed for this was competitive advantage," he adds. "When we saw how much value the retail industry puts on face time, we knew that our competitors wouldn't be beating down the door to do this. When we first started, I figured we had two to three years of competitive differentiation. Now I'm hoping we can stretch that to five. The humanitarian in me says we all need to work this way, but the businessman in me says I'm glad that not everyone has caught on yet."

On Traffic, Acts of Nature, and Taking the Plunge

In an early draft of this book we wanted to conclude with a series of chapters that imagined how the results-only mind-set might be applied outside of the business world. One of the benefits we envisioned was how this new approach to work might reduce traffic congestion and all of its nasty by-products (pollution, fuel costs, road maintenance costs, etc.). If fewer people were required to be at work at a certain time—or at all—then our nation's problems with road capacity, greenhouse gas emissions, and so forth would be less of an issue. Anyone who has ever run errands at 2:00 P.M. on a Tuesday knows that the roads are fine; it's rush hour that's the problem.

In September 2008 we were presented with an opportunity to put these ideas to work. The final data wasn't ready in time for the publication of this update, but the story and the anecdotal results are encouraging. The genesis of this experiment was a grant from the Minnesota Department of Transportation (MNDOT), which allocated money to investigate a variety of solutions to relieving traffic congestion in the Minneapolis–St. Paul metro area.

Our task was to implement ROWE in a number of companies whose employees travel the heavily congested traffic corridors of Interstates 35 and 94. The theory was that if the employees of these companies were no longer beholden to time and place—if the people who worked there could show up when they needed to and not when their boss had previously told them to—then that would relieve congestion.

We already had evidence from our experience with Best Buy that this could work. Their corporate headquarters sits on 494, which is part of the Twin Cities 94 loop. But take the Penn Avenue exit at 8:00 A.M. or 5:00 P.M. and you won't find a line to get in or out of the building. Nor will you find tons of congestion at the intersection. That a major corporate headquarters can leave so slim of a trace on traffic is remarkable. Now it was our job to find out if it's repeatable.

After putting out a call for partners we were fortunate to get a broad variety of companies involved. Valspar, a paint manufacturer, signed up, as well as Fairview Health Services and Hennepin County's Human Services and Public Health Department. For many of the business leaders we collaborated with the MNDOT program was a chance to leverage business innovation in addition to addressing environmental and traffic concerns. Terry Carroll, senior vice president of transformation and chief information officer at Fairview, sees ROWE as part of a larger reform that's needed in his industry.

"Health care is conservative," says Carroll. "My first interest was in creating an environment where we can get more speed. We have an activities-based industry, and we needed an outcomes-based industry. Before ROWE, they did their work in a treadmill environment. Instead of changing how they worked, they just increased the speed and worked harder and harder. It's broken, and it's broken at a time when we need fifty percent more productivity out of people without necessarily expanding capacity. What I wanted to do was to use ROWE to *create* capacity but at the same time give [the] team [a] quality of life that was much better than the life they had today. I wanted both, and both are starting to prove out."

In the following chapter, on how to use the results-only mind-set to manage your people better, we'll hear from Fairview employees who are solving business problems thanks to ROWE. In the meantime, let's look at some of the congestion-mitigation results so far. The Hubert H. Humphrey Institute's interim report found that the average teleworker works remotely 2.4 times per week. They also found that the 2,326 people taking part in the program—of which 2,000 are in a ROWE—are taking 26 percent fewer daily trips to work and 30 percent fewer trips during peak traffic hours. This translates into annual cost savings per worker of $945 and a time savings of over forty-three hours (equal to more than one workweek) of unecessary driving.

This reduction in the impact of commuting comes at an important time. When we first developed ROWE we were two idealistic women working on an island, immersed in a culture that was satisfied with traditional flexible work arrangements and skeptical not only about ROWE, but also about the foundation of our ideas. But since this book was published the conversation has changed. The rest of the world is starting to catch up. First, people are waking up to the fact that the Flexibility Con Game is never going to give people what they need to be happy and productive in the 24/7 global economy. Second, Generation Y continues to put pressure on older generations of workers to stay current with how technology can be used to give people more freedom, more choice, increased connectivity, and new tools for solving problems and getting work done. Third, and perhaps most important of all, there have been a number of world events that have forced the conversation about the limitations of time and physical presence.

For example, in the fall of 2009 the fear of an H1N1 swine flu pandemic got people talking about what would happen if significant portions of the labor force couldn't make it into work, either because they were sick or because they were helping care for sick loved ones. A Harvard School of Public Health report found that only one third of the businesses surveyed believed they could sustain operations without severe problems if half their workforce was absent for two weeks due to H1N1. Less than a quarter (22 percent) of the firms believed they could do so for a month.

Thankfully, H1N1 didn't hit in the way we anticipated, but the scare did encourage some businesses to take a fresh look at their sick leave policies. According to the Harvard study, only about a third of the companies even allowed employees to take time off to take care of sick family members. Less than a quarter offered paid time off in case an employee needed to care for children if their school or day care were closed. Almost half of the businesses still had the antiquated practice of requiring a doctor's note (!) in order for their employees to take sick leave. These kinds of practices are clearly out of touch with the realities of any kind of large-scale crisis, and we were happy to see bloggers and business writers start to think creatively about how organizations could do a better job adapting to forces beyond their control.

A few months later, when a record snowstorm hit the Washington, D.C., area, the federal government got into the conversation. On February 11, 2010, a *Washington Post* article talked about how the snowstorm could advance the cause of telework. The piece cited an August 2009 U.S. Office of Personnel Management report that said that management resistance to teleworking was one of the main obstacles to its adoption by federal workers. Representative Gerald E. Connolly (D–VA) was quoted saying something we've been saying for years. "The biggest barrier to teleworking," he said, "is a cultural mind-set that believes if you are not physically there . . . you must be eating bonbons."

But some offices of the government, such as the U.S. Patent and Trademark Office, found themselves well suited to weathering the storm. According to the agency, more than 80 percent of its eligible staff do some telework. "Telework is considered a business strategy that helps the USPTO achieve its mission and goals," says David Kappos, the agency's director. "At a time when the federal government has been shut down due to inclement weather, our agency has been able to maintain a high level of productivity due to our telework program." John Garing, director of strategic planning and information for the Defense Information Systems Agency, also showed off his ROWE mind-set. "Essentially, the work of the agency goes on," he says, noting that the reason his group has overcome reluctance is because "the work is getting done."

Of course, calling it telework is just another form of Sludge. We shouldn't have *any* labels for work. It's just work, and either it gets done or it doesn't. If we focus on the way the work gets done, then we're missing out on an opportunity to talk about results.

It doesn't have to be this way, even if the stakes seem enormously high. On April 23, 2010, Daniel Gross reported in the online journal *Slate* that when a volcano erupted in Iceland and shut down air traffic all across Europe, California-based Cisco System's acquisition of the Norwegian telecom company Tandberg went on as planned. Well, almost. Instead of flying everyone to one location for a press conference, the two companies used video conferencing to hold a virtual press conference. Suddenly San Jose and Oslo weren't so far apart.

Gross also talked about how some aspects of the European economy—especially those touched by air delivery—had no means of working around the volcano. But like the H1N1 scare and the D.C. snowstorm, this only goes to show how important it is that we're all having the right conversations about work. Leaders, managers, and employees at all levels of business need to talk about how we can free ourselves to cross those boundaries and barriers that largely exist in our minds. What gaps can technology close, and what aspects of our businesses can only happen in the physical world?

Inc. magazine may not have had an Icelandic volcano in mind when they did their virtual work issue for April 2010, but they certainly learned some important lessons about leaving time and physical presence behind. As Max Chafkin, a senior writer for the magazine, joked to the *New York Times*, if he was going to do a piece on virtual work, then maybe the entire magazine staff should work remotely.

"I thought it would involve so much change that it wouldn't be feasible," Mr. Chafkin said.

But Jane Berentson, *Inc.*'s editor, made it a reality. For all of February, the staff of thirty editors, reporters, and producers created the issues outside of their downtown Manhattan office. They used Skype and instant messaging. Speaking to the media, the people who took part in the experiment voiced the usual anxieties about not meeting all the time, but if you compare the issue to any other, you wouldn't be able to tell the difference. As Berentson said to the *Times*, "Why are we in the office in the first place?"

CHAPTER NINE

Managing Using the ROWE Mind-set

n July 2009, we were running a Culture Clinic for Hennepin County's Human Services and Public Health Department, which was part of the MNDOT traffic reduction program we discussed in the previous chapter. The Culture Clinic is the third stage in the ROWE migration, when people get together after the Kickoff and Sludge sessions in order to talk about—and talk through—the challenges they're facing on the day-to-day level as they move from a traditional work environment and into a Results-Only Work Environment. At this stage in the migration people have grown comfortable with the big picture of what a ROWE means, but they are still figuring out what this change means in a practical sense. The Culture Clinic is where managers and teams really start to connect on how to write goals, talk about expectations, take meetings, and relearn the most effective ways to use technologies such as e-mail, voice mail, instant messaging, and so forth.

For this particular Culture Clinic there were twenty people in attendance. A wide variety of employees were represented, including social workers, people who ran the walk-up window for emergency financial aid, and the child support officers. We asked each employee to take a moment and write down the outcome of their job. Then we spent some time with individual groups to see how they responded. When we spoke with the child support group the answer they gave was processing paperwork. Jody pushed back saying that processing paperwork was an activity not an outcome. This comment was met with silence.

"Okay," she said. "What happens if you don't process the paperwork?"

Someone volunteered that then the child-support trial gets delayed.

"Okay, and what happens if the trial gets delayed?"

Someone said that if the trial is delayed then the child support payment doesn't get to the child in time.

"And what happens if the payment doesn't get to the child in a timely way?"

There was another pause, but inside this pause was a growing understanding of what Jody was getting after.

One of the members of the team said, "Then maybe a kid doesn't eat?"

"So let's try this again," said Jody. "What is the outcome of your group?"

Now there was a buzz of excitement. People were connecting with the idea that everything they do was to help ensure the health and welfare of children. Before they were all stuck thinking about the paperwork (aka the activity). Now they were looking at their day-to-day work in terms of the constituency they were serving.

After the Culture Clinic, the manager for this group came up to us with a fresh appreciation for his job. "Why wasn't I thinking about the bigger picture?" he said. "When you asked what my team did, I said that they process paperwork. Now I can't even believe I said that." One of his employees said that for the longest time she had thought of herself as just a peon, but now she realized she had an incredibly important job to do. From that day forward she was going to connect with the importance of that job every day.

Now it would be easy to dismiss this story with a cheap joke about what else would you expect from a government employee. But if you stop to think about the nature of the traditional work environment, you'll see that the workers of Hennepin County are far from alone in their thinking. We would bet there are people on your team who think about their job *entirely* in terms of activities rather than outcomes. In fact, the whole premise of the traditional work environment, with its focus on time and physical presence, is built around activities. Going to meetings is an activity. Stopping by for an update from one of their coworkers is an activity. Reports, forms, replying to e-mails, responding to voice mails, and so on and so forth are all part of a vast sea of activities. You could argue that the very act of getting to work on time is an activity.

Even the most high-achieving individuals have, at some point in their careers, been guilty of focusing on activities instead of outcomes, because that's how the system works. This is not to say that all of these activities are empty, or that none of them are necessary, or that your team is engaged in an entirely fruitless and futile dance that results in zero productivity. (In the case of Hennepin County, that paperwork does need to get done.) Rather, what we're trying to say is that the people limit themselves by focusing on activities instead of on results. The paperwork is the means, not the end.

Thus, it's important for managers to have more meaningful conversations with their employees about driving results. In the following pages you'll hear from genuine ROWE practitioners as they share their wisdom and experience from working in this new way. They represent varied industries and sectors, but they share in common a newfound connection with their work. They have all conquered the transition from a traditional work environment to a ROWE, and they've all transformed themselves from the traditional supervisory role to a more active, engaged coach and mentor role that brings the best out of their employees.

A final note: As we said earlier in this book, being in a Results-Only Work Environment doesn't mean changing what you do. Nor does it mean sacrificing accountability for some humanitarian vision of a happy but ineffective worker. The ideas that follow are instead adjustments you can make to your management style so that your language and behavior reflect a more efficient, focused, and productive approach to work in which the only thing that matters are results. We call it the ROWE mind-set. It's a way of putting on those "blizzard goggles" to see the work in front of you for what it really needs rather than what is required by the mentality of "this is how we've always done things." And while you won't have the total cultural support of a ROWE, what we are about to propose is simple and easy enough that you'll see instant benefits, even if the culture around you is slow in coming around.

Goals, Goals, Goals

Because the traditional work environment is so focused on activities, the shift to basing work on outcomes causes growing pains for managers who migrate to a ROWE. All of the authentic ROWE managers we spoke to shared stories about their particular struggles in figuring out how to work with their employees to create realistic and meaningful (but still ambitious) goals. What follows are some of the best practices that are being employed today.

One idea that we really like was developed in parallel at a number of organizations who migrated into a ROWE after Best Buy, and that is to make all your team members' goals public. In a traditional work environment, people have a general job description, but if you were to ask their coworkers exactly how that job description leads to a particular outcome, it's quite possible you'd be met with a blank stare. That's because a job description is geared toward the activity rather than the result. Often the role of the manager is to coordinate and orchestrate all of his or her employees' job activities and assemble them into a larger outcome, but that can be time consuming and inefficient. This approach also wastes opportunities for natural teamwork.

"Of course we don't publish salaries," says Jeff Gunther, founder and CEO of Meddius, a healthcare integration company. "Public goals allow peers to see what everyone else is doing. People can see where their coworkers need help, where other people's goals and needs dovetail with their own, and where everyone's goals fit into the big picture."

Public goals—which in Meddius's case is displayed through

an internal Web site—also reduce Sludge. "Another benefit is if Sharon is not at a meeting, people don't assume her absence is a negative," Gunther says. "Before you even ask where somebody is, you can check their goals. Does that person even need to be in this meeting? Oftentimes they don't, and their goals reflect that fact."

In general, making goals public increases accountability. No one can hide behind being busy or showing how dedicated they are. There is a standing and open *conversation* about what everyone is working together to achieve. Furthermore, if employees know that everyone's goals are going to be public, then they are more likely to be honest and realistic about what can be accomplished.

So the question then is how to write those goals. Mary Kujawa, manager of packaged solutions 2 at Fairview Health Services, shares how it's important to stay open and fluid when first setting down goals across the team.

"The work has not changed," she says. "Let's start with that. But how do we apply measurable goals? How do you write a goal that captures all the aspects of a job? One thing I've discovered that's helpful is to be aware that jobs have all kinds of components. Some of them are tasky. Some are more personal. Some can even be philosophical. Where do we want to take this aspect of the business? Where do I want to go as a person? There are also some more hard-line business expectations that are nonnegotiable. In our group there are deadlines to be met. There are standards that we don't waver from."

Kujawa also notes that as a manager she has to be aware that everyone has strengths and weaknesses, that everyone has their own style. Organizations that are already taking a strengths-based approach to their employees find a natural ally in ROWE.

"I'm thinking of two people in particular," she says. "One person was a consultant, and then came back to our organization. She has all these process insights that will help make things better for her team in a repeatable, overarching way. That's her strength, and I don't want to get in the way of her ability to innovate. So her goals reflect that.

"On the other side of the coin is an employee who was struggling before ROWE and has been struggling with it since. By nature she needs more attention to detail, so the goals we've written for her are more step-by-step. I'm directing her more and shaping her goals more than I would for the former consultant, but that's okay. Now she can focus and contribute."

Jessica Lawrence, CEO of Girl Scouts of San Gorgonio Council, has this to add. "For us the process of writing results was a pain in the butt," she says. "Most people hadn't had to think about what they did in their job. They just did it. Now we have to be really smart about everything we do. We break them down into loose categories. We make sure to flag the time-sensitive goals, those that have to be done daily, weekly, and monthly. We also have quantitative goals, such as making sure our enrollment meets our standards. Others are more qualitative. I have to make sure we're continually improving our volunteer trainings. One of our manager's jobs is to make sure these trainings are kept fresh, but it's my job to support her effort in a meaningful and measurable way, not just to make sure it gets done."

For a lot of managers, this exercise of writing goals reveals surprising truths about their business. Brad Garland, CEO of the Garland Group, a software development company, talks about how now it seems strange that for so many years he had relied on something as nebulous and ambiguous as a job description. "It used to be that the developers we hired were judged on having a certain skill set," he says. "You need to be able to write in this certain computer language or have that set of previous experience, but there was no indication of proficiency or efficiency. On top of that we used to think of projects in terms of a weekly cycle. But that was only because we had a weekly staff meeting to see where we were on our various projects. We asked people, 'What are you going to do this week?' and they'd report in, and that's how we looked at the work. Employee X has these skills and this is how he's going to use them this week."

"Now that we're ROWE we don't look at work that way," Garland continues. "For one, we realize that the work we do takes place in longer cycles, and the length of that cycle depends a lot on the size and scope of the project. We say we need our results via X date, and it's up to the developers to complete their task by then. We have one developer who never comes into the office on Tuesdays, because that's his magic day for getting things done. We have another who prefers to work on Saturday. Now when we interview people we don't talk about their skill set; we talk about whether or not they feel they can get very specific kinds of work done in a typical cycle. We don't look at work as whether you've got proficiency in a certain language but whether or not you have the ability to apply those skills in a timely way. ROWE has completely changed how we look at outcomes."

Set Them Free

One of the first things that managers discover when they start adopting the ROWE mind-set is that it's important for them to leave their team alone so they can get the job done. Once you've collaborated with your employees to the point where they feel a sense of shared ownership of what needs be done, then the easiest way to kill that trust and momentum is to micromanage.

Michael Reynolds is president and CEO of SpinWeb, a Web site design, development and online marketing firm that migrated to a ROWE in 2008. Michael was one of the early adopters of ROWE, and while the technology sector was already more results-oriented than other industries, he still faced an adjustment. "You have to be patient," he says. "You have to wean yourself off instant gratification. You can't just pop over to someone's cube and ask, 'Is it done yet?' People need to work without interruption."

Mary Frances Moore, vice president of training and adult development at Girl Scouts of San Gorgonio Council, echoes this idea. "What was hardest for me was learning how to plan ahead," she says. "Before ROWE if I wanted a piece of information I would just ask for it the instant I thought of it. Now I'm more focused on the long-term results, so I come up with a list of questions for an employee. It takes away that false sense of urgency. Now nothing is rushed, because most things are anticipated."

Kamille Peterson, IT manager at Fairview Health Services, says that sometimes this means pushing back against employees who want you to be around more, either because that's what they're used to or that is their expectation of what a good manager is. "They wanted me to be more visible," she says, commenting on the reaction of two of her staff members who felt uneasy early on in the migration process. "They said I wasn't in the business enough. They said they didn't feel supported. They wanted me to walk through the halls and show that I was there."

The shift came during Culture Clinic. "We had regular check-in meetings twice a week," she says. "That's at least three hours a week of face time. During Culture Clinic I asked if anyone wanted to get out of our standing meetings. There was only one person who didn't want to, so we canceled every standing meeting. Two weeks later, I admit . . . I was starting to get a little anxious. I felt like I didn't want to contact them, because I didn't want to feel like I didn't trust them. But then gradually my team started to contact me. Within a week everyone had contacted me in a meaningful way, with real questions that needed real answers. No more meaningless check-ins."

As you can imagine, a big part of leaving your team alone is keeping them out of time-wasting meetings. In the traditional work environment, meetings are the ultimate activity. You're bopping along, doing your work, and a problem comes up. If it's a small problem, you send an e-mail. But if the problem has any weight, if it has any size, or if it seems to involve multiple people from multiple departments, then the reflex is to call a meeting. Think about all the times in your workday an issue comes up and the instant, immediate, unthinking reaction is to set up a time to meet. If you're going to take your team from an activities-based group to a results-only group, that reflex has to be eliminated.

We could do a whole book on meetings, but rather than dwell on the topic we will instead share another Hennepin County story from their Culture Clinic. When the group began discussing the "Every meeting is optional" Guidepost, the crowd hit a wall. People in the room said there was "no way in hell" they could make every meeting optional. Jody asked why. Someone said that they have mandated trainings in order to keep their social workers license. The manager from that area spent a lot of time and energy reminding his employees that these trainings were mandatory and attendance was compulsory. He sent around e-mails and left voice-mail messages with people and sent out memos and generally harassed his employees in order to make sure they showed up.

"What happens if you don't go to the meeting?" Jody asked.

Someone volunteered that if they didn't go to the meeting then they wouldn't get licensed.

"What happens if you don't get licensed?"

Another person said that depending on the nature of their casework they wouldn't be allowed to do their job by law.

"And what happens if you can't do your job by law?"

Someone else offered that they'd be fired, and they wouldn't have a job.

"So do you need to be told that these meetings are mandatory?"

Everyone—including the manager who had constantly pestered his employee—agreed that they didn't. They didn't need to be told about basic cause and effect as if they were three-year-olds. Making a meeting mandatory shows your team that you don't trust them. It robs them of the ability to think for themselves, it demotivates them, and it wastes precious time and energy. If you've already been clear about what needs to be done, then get out of the way and let your people work.

When Things Go Wrong in a ROWE

We're not saying that nothing ever goes wrong in a ROWE. A Results-Only Work Environment is still a work environment where people make mistakes, where the unexpected happens, and where the law of unintended consequences is in full effect. The question is how you handle these hiccups.

One of the things we are constantly telling managers in our Manager-only Forums is to address the performance and not the time or physical presence. In a ROWE you would never say "If you're struggling with this task, then maybe you should come in a little earlier all next week." You would never as a manager say "The quality of your work has been down, so I'm going to ask you to start sitting in on the weekly production meeting so you can be more aware of their issues." And you would certainly never start stopping by that person's cube or office just to "make sure everything is going okay."

"You have to be careful," says Brad Garland. "If someone misses their outcomes, they can't automatically face disciplinary action that's time-based. As a manager you have to stop, focus, and evaluate the reason they missed their deliverables. It might have nothing to do with time spent on task. The person might not have been skilled enough to do the job. They may not have had the capacity they needed to do the job. So you have a conversation about it, and you bring up how you're not happy with the result and find out if the person has everything they need to get the job done. For me as a manager, that's why I love ROWE. We're always focused on the work, and if something goes wrong we fix what's concrete rather than something abstract like time."

Debra Hildebrandt, the manager for clinical customer services for Fairview Health Services, says she likes how a Results-Only Work Environment diffuses the inevitable personality conflicts between team members. "When catty things happen, you can really focus on the outcome you're working on without dealing with the peripheral issues," she says. "Sometimes people feel like something gets dumped on them. In brokering this problem I pay less attention to what are you feeling and more attention to what you need. It's just a shade different, but it works. The same goes if coworkers are complaining how So-and-so is 'unprepared' or they're not 'working hard enough.' I've turned my process over to staff. You can continue with this process. You can change it. You have the choice. One group completely changed process. One kept it the same."

Kamille Peterson adds that she tells her employees to simply pretend they are the manager of their own area. "I tell them you're the expert," she says. "You know what you think is best. It's not like you can flip a switch and turn off the whole company."

A Final Thought

For managers, the biggest change in moving from a traditional work environment to a ROWE is in recognizing the difference between activities and outcomes. This isn't always as easy as it seems. As we all know, the business day flies by, and because of the incredible intensity of work, it can be hard to take a moment to pause the action and ask whether or not what you're doing is important to the larger mission. Furthermore, as we noted in the opening story about Hennepin County, all those tasks and activities have their place. The question is what you reward.

"One of the things I role modeled with my HR team was shifting the focus in their goals from how much they did to the impact of what they did," says Gap vice president of HR Eric Severson. He notes that even when you tie a project or action to higher-level organizational goals, it's easy to see the goals themselves as measures only of getting the project done. "As a result, in order to get the best review rating possible, people would often strive to complete as many projects as possible, and to add extra projects for extra credit," says Severson. "The result was that many employees were focused on how much they did rather than if their work actually had a measurable and desirable impact on the business."

Over the past two years Severson and his team have evolved a model for planning and assessing performance. This goal-setting and -measuring program identifies and emphasizes HR outcomes, such as employee engagement and customer service scores and stakeholder feedback responses, to be improved. The completion of projects is emphasized less, and now comprises a smaller percentage of their job performance rating.

"We want people to be rewarded for getting results rather than for being busy," says Severson. "Because an employee's review score is based much more on quantitative measures like employee engagement and customer service than on project completion, employees are motivated to do what whatever it takes to drive those scores, even if it means stopping projects that the business is losing interest in midstream and changing course or putting planned initiatives on the back burner when more important business needs surface.

"In short, this is making my team more flexible, just in time, and responsive to the business, because employees aren't worried about getting dinged on their reviews at the end of the year for not completing a project that was listed on their goals a year earlier. Instead, they know that they have the freedom (with the right partnership and communication) and my support to do whatever it takes to get results, rather than adhering slavishly to project goals for their own sake."

A final thought on the ideas in this chapter.

We love hearing how managers adapt to a ROWE, because even though there are commonalities, each manager finds his or her own unique solutions to their own unique problems. Some of these solutions are fantastically creative. Others are plain and pragmatic. Still others seem like only minor adjustments to business as usual and yet have profound results.

What's important here is not necessarily the inherent quality of these solutions but the deeper change behind them. Before a manager can innovate using these ideas, they first had to adopt the ROWE mind-set. ROWE is not something you apply or dabble in, or try on for a while. You have to embrace it. (Even if the workplace that surrounds you isn't ready yet.)

So our final plea to you is to change your mind about work. Take one final look at the old, outdated attitudes and beliefs of the traditional work environment and tell yourself that you're done with them. There's a better way of working, and even if you don't know exactly what the day to day of that means yet, it's better than what you're doing now.

Epilogue

Y ou have the right to control your time.

You have the right to eat when you're hungry and sleep when you're tired.

It's that simple. Yes, your company is providing you with a paycheck and possibly other benefits. Yes, they are giving you a job, and, in some cases, a career. For that you absolutely, positively owe them hard work, focus, and dedication. More important, you owe them real, measurable results. But if you're delivering those results, and your company is benefiting, then there is no reason why they should have the right to make you sit in a cubicle from eight to five. You owe them your work; you do not owe them your time. You do not owe them your life.

For us this line of thinking is irrefutable. We have heard every objection imaginable to the *logistics* of creating a Results-Only Work Environment, but we have yet to hear a single person stand up and say that adults don't deserve to be treated like adults.

Nevertheless, social change happens slowly and not without resistance. Even commonsense ideas have to be argued over before they are implemented. It's not as if one day some-one said, "Hey, maybe seven-year-olds shouldn't work in coal mines," and the country nodded its collective head in agreement and the next day we had child labor laws. History is filled with people who have dedicated their lives to being on the wrong side of an argument.

History also teaches us that work can change. If you were to travel back in time and tell someone at the beginning of the last century that women would enter the workplace in record numbers, that there would be federally mandated health and safety regulations, that technology would allow people to conduct business twenty-four hours a day, they would have thought you were crazy. We wonder what a time traveler from a hundred years from now would tell us that we wouldn't believe, but a Results-Only Work Environment would not surprise us in the least. The next generation of employees will have grown up with too much control over their time to give it up for the sake of a job.

At the same time, we have a fight on our hands, and we're asking for everyone's help. The change from a traditional work environment to a Results-Only Work Environment will come from the middle and below. As a result it will not come easily or quickly. We're grateful to those brave souls in upper management who pushed for ROWE from above. We also realized very early in this process that the people typically identified as leaders—the ones with the weighted business cards and impressive titles—weren't necessarily going to fight this fight. The people have to demand a better way of working and living. No one is going to give this to us.

Everyone has a role to play. As we converted Best Buy employees team by team to a Results-Only Work Environment, we found that it was the people's passion for the new lifestyle that in turn spawned hundreds of evangelists who continue to carry the change forward. But everyone evangelizes differently. Some shout it from the rooftops. Others lead quietly by example. Still others follow with conviction.

Regardless of how you decide to participate it's not going to be an easy path to walk. You're going to need help and support from the people around you, because you'll find resistance all along the way. There is no end to the battles that need to be fought and obstacles that need to be overcome. There will be moments every day when you'll think, "It would be so much easier to just forget about this and not fight anymore."

When these moments come, know that you are not alone. Right now we are out in the world working to make ROWE a reality. We're speaking to any audience that will listen, meeting with business leaders and government officials. We're doing all of this because:

There is a better way to work.
A ROWE can have a positive impact on quality of life
     (and drive business results) for *everyone*.
People have the right to control their time.

We hope you say yes to this cause. Say yes to fighting for control over your time. Even though you may get booed instead of cheered, even though you may never hear applause, say yes to making this new way of living and working a reality.

And if you can't say yes to fighting for a results-only world, at least say yes to the idea. Say yes because there are people around you who are doing everything they can to make this change. Say yes now so when the time comes you'll be ready to join us.

How ROWE Are You?

1. If people in my organization think a particular meeting is a waste of time, they:

   A. start answering e-mails on their laptop and ignore everything else that's going on.
   B. catch the meeting organizer after the meeting and ask what they were trying to accomplish.
   C. stop the meeting and ask the facilitator what they are hoping to accomplish.

2. When a work process at my company is improved and waste is removed from the system, the time saved is replaced by:

   A. employees sitting in their cubes until five because that is when the workday is over.
   B. management immediately giving employees more work.
   C. whatever activities the employees feel are valuable, perhaps personal time, developmental projects, assisting teammates, etc.

3. If someone at my company wants to work from home on a Tuesday, they:

   A. would need to ask their boss for permission, and inform their team members and customers.
   B. would need to inform their team and customers.
   C. wouldn't need to ask permission or inform anyone.

4. When a meeting is set up at my company, the expectation is:

   A. you will be physically present in a meeting room at the office building.
   B. if you have an acceptable excuse, you are allowed to call in to the meeting.
   C. you will deliver what you need to deliver, regardless of location.

5. At my company, when we're sick and do work from home:

   A. we put in eight hours of sick time or paid time off (PTO).
   B. we put in four hours of sick time or PTO.
   C. we don't submit any sick time or PTO.

6. Vacation time at my organization is allotted:

   A. by years of service.
   B. by years of service, and we can donate time to employees who have atypical needs for leave.
   C. our vacation time or PTO is unlimited.

7. If someone at my company needs to attend a funeral they:

    A. submit personal time or PTO.

    B. use bereavement leave time.

    C. just go and don't submit any time.

8. If asked what work "looks like," people at my company would say:

    A. a person sitting in a cube, typing on a keyboard.

    B. a person conducting a meeting in a conference room.

    C. work doesn't have a particular "look." Work can be happening at any time, so it's hard to tell what it looks like.

9. When my coworkers say "I'm off to work," their friends and families think:

    A. They must be headed to the company office building.

    B. They will be in their home office or the company office building.

    C. I have no idea where they're going.

10. Where I work, employees are expected to arrive at the office to start the workday:

    A. no later than 7:30 AM.

    B. between 8:00 AM and 9:00 AM.

    C. whenever they want; they may not even come to the office to do work.

11. At our company, leaving the workplace at 3:00 PM is acceptable if you:

   A. came into the office at 6:00 AM and only took a thirty-minute lunch break.
   B. came in at your regular time but have a doctor appointment that afternoon.
   C. are breathing and delivering results that meet expectations.

12. At my company, recognition is most often given for:

   A. working long hours.
   B. taking on the tough projects, whether they get completed or not.
   C. delivering results.

13. Where I work, an exempt (salaried) employee works, on average:

   A. a minimum of forty to fifty hours a week.
   B. about forty hours a week, but it fluctuates according to business rhythms.
   C. Not sure; we don't track hours for our exempt employees.

14. At my company, when a meeting invite is received we:

   A. accept immediately—every meeting is important.
   B. review the invite and accept or decline—usually based on who sent the invite.
   C. review the invite and accept or decline—based on the goal and whether a meeting is the best way to accomplish it.

15. In my organization, conference calls are:

   A. very rare—we almost always operate with face-to-face meetings.

   B. fairly common, but only to do business with people out of town.

   C. widely acceptable—all meeting invites include the option to call in.

16. In my organization:

   A. we take care of personal errands outside of core work hours.

   B. we submit 'personal time' to run errands.

   C. we can do whatever we want without asking permission.

17. At our company, the only acceptable reasons to leave work are:

   A. things like doctor appointments, dentist appointments, or day care issues.

   B. Almost any reason is okay as long as you explain it to your manager and team.

   C. Our employees are free to come and go as they please without any explanation.

18. At our company, blocking a day every week as "No Meeting Day" would be viewed as:

   A. a great way to get work done without distractions.

   B. a nice idea, but everyone would know it wouldn't work.

   C. unnecessary because everyone is in control of when and how they work.

19. At my company, core work hours are:

    A. Monday through Friday, 8:00 AM to 5:00 PM.
    B. Monday through Friday, 10:00 AM to 2:00 PM.
    C. We don't have core work hours.

20. When someone at our company schedules a doctor ap-
    pointment, they are likely to:

    A. schedule the appointment outside of core work hours.
    B. notify their manager, teammates, and employees when
       they'll be unavailable.
    C. simply schedule the appointment for whenever it works
       best and go.

21. If a *major* fire drill happens and lands on an employee's desk:

    A. they react immediately and stay as long as it takes to
       get the fire drill taken care of.
    B. they react to the fire drill and involve the appropriate
       resources to reach a well-informed decision.
    C. the team and employee react to the fire drill but in-
       form the requester of the risks involved in making
       hasty decisions, and focus on what can be done to pre-
       vent this emergency from recurring.

22. If a *perceived* fire drill happens and lands on an employee's
    desk:

    A. they react immediately and stay as long as it takes to
       get the fire drill taken care of even though they don't
       think the need is urgent.
    B. they react to the fire drill but inform the requester of
       the risks involved in making hasty decisions.

C. they respectfully push back on the cause of the fire drill and ask questions to determine the real priority of the work.

23. If an employee at my organization arrives at the office at noon:

A. a coworker or manager will ask them, "Where have you been? Did you have a doctor appointment?"
B. they will receive some questioning looks.
C. coworkers will say "Hello!"

24. If an employee at my company sends e-mail at 2:00 AM:

A. their manager will ask them why they were up working so late.
B. their manager will wonder why they were working so late, but not say anything about it.
C. their manager will not notice what time the e-mail was sent; they will only pay attention to the content and effectiveness.

Answer key:

If you answered all or mostly A's: You are not alone. You are in a typical work environment. Employees may often complain about lack of control over work-life balance. Work is getting done, but not always in the most efficient manner. Top performers may be leaving the organization in search of a healthier balance between work and life. ROWE can infuse your organization with tremendous energy and focus, improving business results. Focus on removing Sludge from the environment. The language most often used in a traditional work environment is focused on time. Focusing your language on results and outcomes will kick-start your organization into becoming a Results-Only Work Environment.

If you answered all or mostly B's: You are in a work environment with some flexibility. You may have programs available (job sharing, telecommuting, flextime, etc.) to help provide a level of flexibility, but people are still complaining about a lack of control. ROWE will take your organization to the next level of productivity and improve the employee experience. Focusing on only results by creating results-based job descriptions, goals, and performance development creates the opportunity for people to be fully engaged, invested, proactive, productive, and passionate.

If you answered all or mostly C's: Congratulations! You work in a forward-thinking environment, dedicated to working productively and enjoying life outside of work. Continue to focus on results and help spread the word!

Yeah, Buts

"People will take advantage and slack off."

First, people are taking advantage and slacking off now. The reason you can't tell is that you're measuring them with a combination of results and time. In a ROWE, if you don't get results then you don't get to keep your job. The slackers either shape up or they get fired. Meanwhile, the good employees work even harder because they are being rewarded with control over their time.

"How can you ever reach anybody if they're not in the office?"

People are more reachable now than they ever have been in human history. People have cell phones. They are on e-mail. They don't need a workstation. They don't need a phone with a cord that plugs into the wall to be reachable. In a ROWE if you need to reach someone you e-mail them or you call them. But here is another thought: When you're clear about timetables, outcomes, and expectations, a lot of those spontaneous requests dry up. You start to anticipate your own questions. You plan better so you have fewer emergencies. You don't casually stop by someone's office and interrupt their work so you can get the answer to one question. You work with more purpose.

"But what if you really, really, really need to reach somebody?"

Have you tried their cell phone? Have you sent them an e-mail? Have you tried someone else on their team? Is it a question you can answer yourself with a little more effort? We're so used to filling the hours that we can't think for ourselves. It's like when someone asks you a question about what's going on in the news when they could go online and get the answer for themselves. Your coworkers and colleagues aren't there to be your search engine/file cabinet/dictionary. If it's a real emergency, then there is probably more than one person you need help from. And if there is only one person who can answer any question in an organization, then that is an organizational problem, not the fault of the person who isn't available.

"A manager needs to be there for people."

There are a lot of managers who genuinely care about their employees. Just as important, there are managers out there who have built their identity on showing that they care. "I need to be there for my people," they say. "My people count on me." But there is more to being there for someone than physical presence. You can still be there for your people by giving them clear goals and expectations. You can be there by coaching their development, removing obstacles that fall in their path. Perhaps the best way to be there for them is to leave them alone and trust them to do their job.

"What if I get stuck with more work than anybody else?"

In a traditional work environment people can feel unsupported and underappreciated. You look around and see people who don't produce and get paid more. It's easy to feel like a victim. On the practical side, a ROWE gives you the right to question the work you're doing. If your manager sets unrealistic expectations or piles on too much work, then that isn't good for anyone. In a ROWE it's your job to stand up for what best serves the business and the customer. On the emotional side, you find yourself not focusing on how other people spend their time. You do your job and you enjoy your freedom, and what other people do becomes their business.

"We're already doing this; this isn't anything new."

Show us one work environment that doesn't have Sludge in it and we'll eat our book.

"If everyone becomes more efficient are there going to be layoffs."

Some people can sense the enormity of a ROWE and it scares them. People at all levels fear that they will find out the truth about their organization: that a team is bloated; that there are managers who have no business managing people. But is the fear of the truth a good reason to resist what is otherwise positive change? If your organization is bloated and top-heavy or overstaffed or undertrained or misguided, then yes a ROWE could reveal those truths. But most people know what's wrong with their company already; there just isn't any incentive for change. There can be some growing pains with a ROWE, but isn't a sane work environment ultimately worth it?

"How can you advance your career if no one sees you working?"

This sounds like the kind of worry that keeps people from participating in current flexible-work arrangements. People fear that if they're not putting in enough face time, then they won't get credit for the work. First, a ROWE doesn't mean that no one ever sees anyone ever again, or that everyone works at home. Don't worry—people will see you do your thing. But more important, you will be measured more for actual performance than perceived performance. If you're given a goal and you meet that goal, then that is what will advance your career whether anyone sees you (with their eyes) do it or not. You get ahead through actual achievement, not by simply *looking* like you're an achiever.

"Isn't it unprofessional to answer a customer's question while you're shopping?"

First of all, they don't have to know. This is Sludge Anticipation. You're worried that people are going to judge you because a person who is out shopping can't also be working. If you answer the person's question in a professional manner then why tell them where you are? Honestly, they don't care. They want your help, not an update on your personal life.

"What if somebody is out of the office for a whole month? Isn't it just common courtesy to let people know where you are?"

A funny thing happens when we talk about a ROWE. We'll say to people, "You can do whatever you want, whenever you want, as along as the work gets done," and it's like their brains get all fried by the first part of that sentence and they don't even hear the "as long as the work gets done" part. If you go to Hawaii for a whole month and you fail to deliver your outcomes, then you will be fired. If you don't do your job, you don't get to keep your job. But if you want to be out of the state or out of the country for a month and you can still meet your deliverables, then that's fine. You have to tell people where you are so they can conference you in for a meeting, for example. But as long as the work gets done, you don't have to beg for permission to be gone.

"This will work for some people but not everyone. Some people simply need more supervision."

People don't need supervision. They need a clear idea of what they need to do and a clear sense of when it needs to be done. If you call your deli and ask them to deliver you a delicious turkey sandwich in the next half hour, you don't need to then go down there to watch them make it and follow the delivery guy back to your office. You trust that they are going to deliver on expectations. And if they don't deliver a delicious turkey sandwich in a half hour then you have two choices: complain and hope that service improves, or switch delis.

"How will we know if work is getting done if we can't see people?"

How do you know now? In today's economy people work

with information. They talk on the phone. They type on their computers. If you walk by a row of cubicles you don't know for a fact the occupants are actually working or if they're just looking busy. In a ROWE you know the work is getting done because you've been crystal-clear about goals and expectations. X is to be delivered to Y on such-and-such a date. If people don't deliver the work, you know immediately and can act accordingly.

"Relationships are so important. What will happen to relationships?"

Relationships are important. And relationships will be fine. We assume that we're improving relationships with people because we're all in the same building together. But being together doesn't guarantee that people are connecting. In a ROWE people work on their relationships with more purpose. Because you can't assume people will be around, you make career development, mentoring, and coaching a part of the results to be delivered. No more taking people for granted.

"How can you schedule meetings if you don't know when people are working?"

In a ROWE you can no longer casually schedule a meeting. You don't schedule meetings based around time. You schedule meetings based on outcome. If the outcome requires that people attend, then they will attend. If they don't need to be there in person they can send a representative, or they can provide the information they're supposed to deliver ahead of time.

"How will we know if salaried employees are putting in forty hours?"

You don't know. And it doesn't matter. In a ROWE you measure someone's performance based on results. You tell them what they're supposed to do and they either deliver or they don't. Time is not a factor. People start performing rather than putting in time.

"What about teams?"

Teams are overrated. In a ROWE people stop teaming because they feel obligated to team. No more teaming for the sake of teaming, because it's fashionable or expected. People team up because the outcome requires it. In fact, teams get much stronger in a ROWE because there is natural cross training. Because you can't assume that people are going to be in the office (including you) teammates make sure they can support one another in an emergency.

"What if everyone decides not to work at the same time?"

That depends. Does the job require that people work at the same time? Because if the outcome doesn't demand that everyone work at the same time, then the answer is "That's fine." But if the job requires certain people to be together or to coordinate their efforts at the same time, then that's what they have to do. ROWE gives employees power over how they work and when they work, but they still have to work. They are still responsible for serving the customer, whether that customer is internal or external. That sense of responsibility—coupled with the power to meet those responsibilities however they want—actually breeds higher performance. People don't even think about blowing off work in a ROWE.

"If there's no line between work and life, how will I keep from overworking?"

In a ROWE you don't overwork, because there is no incentive to overwork. You aren't getting rewarded for putting in more hours. You are no longer a hero for pulling an all-nighter or being the first one through the door in the morning or working on the weekend. You're only rewarded for delivering results. Once you've delivered those results, you stop working and do something else. It's nice.

ACKNOWLEDGMENTS

This book is our way of saying that there really is a better way to work, a better way to live. It started in 2001 when we set out to pave a new path for workers everywhere. A spark was ignited at the corporate headquarters of Best Buy with a handful of brave and spirited employees. It took courage, perseverance, and a whole lot of guts to buck the status quo and make a ROWE grow and take hold. We proved people really *can* be trusted, and that business and people thrive in this new environment. We proved that the old rules and policies are ludicrous. We proved that it no longer makes sense to create fancy flavor-of-the-month programs to make people feel better for a while. We proved that changing the game is the only game. And that the new standard is a ROWE.

So first, to the pioneers at Best Buy who have successfully created the new standard—the blueprint—for ROWE. Your stories are an inspiration to others who want a better life. Your stories prove that ROWE isn't just a theory, but a reality. Your stories are the motivation for others who want to change the status quo. Thank you for believing in us, and for being a beacon of hope for all workers.

To John Larson and Natalie Burns at Bright House, Inc.,

who infuse our lives with energy and excitement every day—together, we will rock the world! We're so thankful that you are part of the journey.

To our writer, Dennis Cass. You got into our heads, found our voice, and made ROWE come to life on the printed page. For this, we will be forever grateful.

To Adrian Zackheim, Adrienne Schultz, Will Weisser, and the team at Portfolio—thank you for taking us on and challenging us along the way. You made it possible for us to tell our story to the world.

To the CultureRx team—thank you for weathering the storm with us and for your determination to help make ROWE the status quo.

Jody's Special Thanks

To my parents, George and Beverly Hartzell, who instilled in me a spirit of courage and perseverance; who believed that whatever needed to get done could get done; and who believed if anyone could make a splash, I could.

To my husband, David Thompson—who through tears, rants, and raves, stays patiently by my side.

To my children, Elliot and Colin Kohl. Life doesn't have to be about all work and no play—do what you love. Never settle.

Cali's Special Thanks

To my parents, Heidi and José Gaibor—you raised me to stand up for what I believe in and to be confident that I would be successful in anything I put my mind to. I learned to dream big from you, and I learned that if something isn't right, it just takes one voice to start paving a new path.

To my husband and best friend, Marty Ressler—who has seen and listened to every emotion this movement provokes in me, from exasperation to pure joy. Your devotion to me and our family, and my always knowing you'll have my back, means so much to me.

To my three little munchkins, Trystan, Jackson, and Keaton—who remind me every day that happiness comes from the simplest things. You inspire me to continue fighting the fight so when you grow up, you'll never know the games that used to make up the world of work.

To my brother, Jesse Gaibor, who has been my friend and supporter in every task I've undertaken. Thank you for your advice and your encouragement. I'm lucky to have you in my life.

To my grandfather Bob Hoeppner—you taught me that if I keep trying, I *will* succeed. I learned my "Don't give up" lessons from you, and they come in handy quite often!

To the rest of my family—my grandmother, aunts, uncles, cousins, and in-laws. Thank you for your support and encouragement throughout my life. I'm very fortunate to have such a big, loving cheering section!

To my friends—thank you for listening to, and sometimes going through with me, the ups and downs of this chaotic, sometimes frustrating, exhilarating, life-altering movement. I look forward to having you by my side for many, many more years.

INDEX

Adaptive change
   difficulty of, 80
   elements of, 75
   self-adjustment in, 91
   and ROWE, 75-78, 91
Administrative assistants, 109
Alternative Work Program (AWP),
      45–48
   flextime arrangements in, 5
   positive impact of, 45
   and Sludge, 46–48
Attitude change, process of, 74–75,
      162–63

Back Sludge, 49, 52–53, 59, 163
Berentson, Jane, 193
Best Buy
   Alternative Work Program, 4–5,
      45–48
   ROWE, positive impact of, 6, 188,
      198
   See also Results-Only Work
      Environment (ROWE)
Bloomberg, Michael, 13–14, 21, 23

Calendar exercise, 63–65
Career advancement, and ROWE, 194
Carroll, Terry, 188–89
Chafkin, Max, 192–93

Change
   adaptive change, 75–77, 80
   in attitude, examples of, 74–75,
      162–63
   best practices, ROWE rejection of,
      76–77
   culture as factor, 46–47, 75
   loss associated with, 80
   Sludge eradication, 55–60, 97–98,
      139–50
   sustaining, problem of, 78–79
   technical change, 75–78
   in traditional work environment,
      74, 179
   traditional work to ROWE
      transition, 74–77
Cisco system, 192
Coach, ROWE manager as, 128,
      192–93
College students, compared to
      ROWE participants, 66–67
Communication
   increase and ROWE, 112, 119, 129,
      172
   reaching others, methods of, 129,
      191–92
Connolly, Rep. Gerald E., 191
Control, sense of
   control-demand as force, 33–35

Control, sense of (*continued*)
   and day-off activities, 33–34, 103
   flexible schedule misconception, 69
   illusion of control, 44
   increased and ROWE, 34–35,
      79–80, 103, 118, 147, 170
   and Sludge, 32
   TiVo example, 79
Creativity
   clock, negative influence of, 19
   and knowledge workers, 16
Cross training, and teams, 102, 197
Culture of company
   and instituting change, 46–47, 75
   meetings, significance of, 125–26
CultureRx study, 156–61

Demands
   control-demand as force, 33-35
   and flexible schedule, 69
   as negative force, 33–35
   types of, 33
Drive-by, 127

Emergencies
   reaching others, methods of, 129,
      223–24
   and ROWE, 127–28
   traditional workplace, 126–27
Employee manuals, 173
Entrepreneurs, compared to ROWE,
   150–51
Excuses
   lack of and ROWE, 154
   in traditional work environment,
      99–100, 154

Fair Labor Standards Act (1938), 15
Fairview Health Services, 188–89,
   199, 202, 206
   Culture Clinic, 203
Family Medical Leave Act, 108

Fear
   and bloated organizations, 225–26
   and management migration,
      171–72
   Sludge Anticipation, 49–50, 58–59,
      163, 226
Federal regulations, and ROWE,
   73*n*, 96*n*, 108
Fire drills, 126–27
Flexible schedules
   Alternative Work Program, 5,
      45–48
   company-imposed restrictions,
      40–42, 69
   control-demand in, 69
   Flexibility Con Game, 44–45,
      68–69
   flex-worker, perception of, 42–43
   management concerns about, 81
   negative judgments about. *See*
      Sludge
   compared to ROWE, 69
   trust issues, 42–43
   types of arrangements, 5
Flexible Work and Well-Being
   Center, 156–58

Gap Inc. Outlet, 183–87
Garing, John, 191–92
Garland Group, 201
Garland, Jeff, 201
Girl Scouts of San Gorgonio
   Council, 179–83, 200, 202
Goals/expectations, setting, 121, 153,
   200, 228
Gross, Daniel, 192
Guideposts. *See* 13 Guideposts
Guilt
   absence and ROWE, 95, 140, 147,
      149
   Sludge-related, 32, 37, 45, 54, 58,
      64

traditional workplace, examples of,
78
Gunther, Jeff, 198

Harvard School of Public Health,
190
Hennepin County Culture Clinic,
194–97, 204
Hennepin County Human Services
and Public Health Department,
188, 194–97, 207
Hildebrandt, Debra, 206
Hourly employees, in ROWE, 73*n*,
96*n*
How ROWE Are You?, 215–22
Hubert H. Humphrey Institute, 189

Information/service-based economy
beliefs about work not revelant to,
23–28
intellectual requirements for, 16

Job descriptions, 24
Judging others
about time/work. *See* Sludge
forms of, 29–30

Kappos, David, 191
Keep America Beautiful, 74–75
Kelly, Erin, 156–58
Kickoff, 88
Knowledge workers, intellectual
requirements of, 16
Kujawa, Mary, 199–200

Lateness
lack of and ROWE. *See* Time and
ROWE
Sludge Anticipation, 49–50
traditional view, 11–12, 20
Lawrence, Jessica, 180–83, 200
Leadership meetings, 90

Lunch hour, traditional workplace,
92

Malyszka, Daniel, 180
Management, traditional
common problems of, 9–10
management by walking around,
25, 172, 174
modified ROWE practiced by, 172
outdated beliefs about, 24
as parent role, 171, 174
and Sludge, 171
top-down model, 164
Management and ROWE
coaching role of, 128, 224–25
communication, level of, 128
concerns about, 107, 152–54, 168
inspiring others, 164–65
leading versus managing, 130, 154,
171–72
migration to ROWE, 91, 171–72
no schedules, adjustment to, 107
13 Guideposts, introducing to,
90, 181
tips for, 172–74
and trust, 174, 225
Meddius, 198–99
Meeting(s)
mandatory attendance, 90–91
negative aspects of, 27
No-Meeting Wednesdays, 77–79
Meetings and ROWE
attendance as optional, 98–99, 122,
181, 228
cancelled, 122–23
positive impact of, 125
questioning value of, 123–25
scheduling, basis of, 203–4, 228
by speakerphone, 107
Migration to ROWE
administrative assistants, absence
from, 109

Migration to ROWE (*continued*)
  management migration, 90, 171–72
  process/topics of, 55, 88
  resistance to ROWE, 115
  13 Guideposts, use of, 91
  traditional work to ROWE
    transition, 74–77
Minnesota Department of
  Transportation (MNDOT), 188
Moen, Phyllis, 156–58
Moore, Mary Francis, 202

New-age companies, origin of, 26
No-Meeting Wednesdays, 77–79

Overseas business, non-traditional
  methods, 27
Overwork, ROWE and lack of,
  147–49, 157–58, 230

Parents
  ROWE, benefits of, 175–77
  as workers, negative comments
    about, 28–29, 31, 57, 173
Peck, Art, 185
Peterson, Kamille, 202, 206
Presenteeism, 17–20
  elements of, 17–18
  lack of and ROWE, 118–19
  negative aspects of, 18–20
Priorities, work and ROWE, 131–32
Productivity, increase and ROWE, 6,
  101, 120, 135, 153–54

Responsibility, increase and ROWE,
  101, 112, 120, 229
Ressler, Cali, 4–5, 20–21, 46, 76
Results-Only Work Environment
  (ROWE)
  adaptive change related to, 75–78,
    91
  best practices, rejection of, 76–77

and career advancement, 226
as cause, advancing for future,
  162–70, 212–13
as companywide culture, 71
control, increase for participants,
  34–35, 79–80, 103, 118, 147,
  170
criticisms of, 67–68, 168
CultureRx study, 156–61
defined, 3–4, 66
employee/employer as winners, 82
employee problems, handling of,
  172–73
evolution of, 4–6
guilt, absence of, 95, 140, 147, 149
How ROWE Are You?, 215–22
Kickoff, 88
management. *See* Management and
  ROWE
meetings in. *See* Meetings and
  ROWE
and new employees, 120
parents, benefits for, 175–77
as people's movement, 170–71
personal accounts of, 9–10, 37–38,
  61–62, 83–86, 111–13, 133–36,
  152–55, 175–77
personal responsibility, increase in,
  101, 112, 120, 229
person-level, positive impact on, 7,
  82
versus Results-Oriented Work
  Environment, 65–66, 179
salary/rewards, basis of, 4, 71–72,
  105, 149, 173
scalability of, 118
Sludge, eradicating, 55–60, 87,
  97–98, 139–50, 162–64
social aspects, 146
stress/overwork, lack of, 148–49,
  157–58, 230
13 Guideposts, 87–93

time, use of. *See* Time and ROWE
transition to. *See* Migration to
   ROWE
and trust, 113, 121–22, 181
turnover-rates, 118, 158–60
underperformers, impact on, 121,
   152–53
work accomplished. *See* Work and
   ROWE
Rewards. *See* Salary
Reynolds, Michael, 202

Salary/rewards, ROWE, basis of, 4,
   71–72, 105, 149, 173
Self-employment, compared to
   ROWE, 150–51
Severson, Eric, 183–87, 207–8
Slackers, absence in ROWE, 118, 223
Sludge
   and Alternative Work Program,
      46–48
   Back Sludge, 49, 52–53, 59, 163
   business-as-battle metaphor,
      138–39
   as control tactic, 32–33
   eradicating, process of, 55–60,
      97–98, 139–50, 162–64, 181
   and flexible schedule, 44–45
   Guideposts related to, 140
   and guilt, 32, 37, 45, 54, 58, 64
   from management, 171
   meaning of, 30, 47
   negative comments, examples of,
      30–31, 45–47, 51–53, 57
   negative impact of, 31–32, 47–48,
      50–54
   and public goals, 198–99
   ROWE, absence in, 37–38
   Sludge Anticipation, 49–50, 58–59,
      163, 226
   Sludge Conspiracy, 49, 52–54, 59,
      163

   Sludge Justification, 49, 51–52,
      56–57, 163
   Sludge Resignation, 139
   Sludge sessions, 48–49, 87
   underlying messages in, 32, 53,
      57–58, 60
Social activities, and ROWE, 146
Sociological study of ROWE
   (CultureRx), 156–61
SpinWeb, 202
Strategic Alliance team, 46
Stress
   good stress, 148
   ROWE and lack of, 147–49,
      157–58, 230
Studio approach, elements of, 85
Summer Hours programs, 24
Syngal, Sonia, 185

Tandberg, 192
Teams and ROWE
   and cross training, 102, 229
   natural formation of, 128–29, 229
   studio approach, 85
Technical change
   elements of, 75–76
   example of, 76
   No-Meeting Wednesday's
      example, 77–79
13 Guideposts, 87–93, 181
   development of, 88
   listing of, 89
   and management, 90
   and migration process, 91
   related to Sludge eradication, 140
   related to time, 93, 140
   related to work, 116
Thompson, Jody, 5–6, 46, 77
Time and ROWE
   calendar exercise, 63–65
   clock, new relationship to, 93–98
   CultureRx results on, 157–58

Time and ROWE (*continued*)
  every day as Saturday, 150–51
  and federal regulations, 73*n*, 96*n*,
    108
  compared to flextime, 69
  Guideposts related to, 93, 140
  hours worked, lack of talk about,
    144–47
  management adjustment to, 107
  new rules about, 93–110
  nonexempt employees in, 73*n*, 96*n*
  overtime work, implication of,
    145
  time management, concept of,
    94–95
  time-off, unlimited, 85–86, 105–7,
    133–35, 149, 227
  typical worker day, examples of,
    84–86, 103
  workers compared to college
    students, 66–67
Time-work relationship
  creativity stifled by, 19
  judging others about. *See* Sludge
  legal regulation of, 15
  lunch hour, 92
  myth about, 13–15
  new conception of. *See* Results-
    Only Work Environment
    (ROWE); Time and ROWE
  "on time," beliefs about, 71
  outdated attitudes, 19–23
  Presenteeism, 17–20
  time management, 94
  vacation leave, 84, 104–6
TiVo, 79, 103
Trust
  and flexible schedule, 42–43
  increase and ROWE, 113, 121–22
  by management, 174, 225
Turnover rates, and ROWE, 118,
  158–60

U.S. Office of Personnel
    Management, 191
U.S. Patent and Trademark Office,
    191

Vacation
  ROWE, unlimited time off,
    85–86, 105–7
  in traditional work environment,
    104–6, 161
Valspar, 188

War, business-as-battle metaphor,
    137–39
Work, traditional
  bloated organizations, 225–26
  business-as-battle metaphor,
    137–39
  busy work, 130
  change, mechanics of, 74, 76
  control-demand, as negative force,
    33–35
  drive-by, 127
  employee manuals, 173
  evil corporate America image,
    83–84
  excuses, use of, 49–50, 56, 99–100,
    154
  fire drills, 126–27
  judging others at. *See* Sludge
  management. *See* Management,
    traditional
  meetings. *See* Meeting(s)
  negative aspects of, 2, 12–13
  new culture of. *See* Results-Only
    Work Environment (ROWE)
  outdated beliefs about, 23–28
  and physical space, 116–17
  redesign of, 158
  and technical change, 75–76
  time, conception of. *See* Time-
    work relationship

Work and ROWE
  communication, increase in, 112,
      119, 129, 172
  emergencies, handling of,
      127–28
  goals/expectations, setting, 121,
      153, 228
  Guideposts related to, 116
  and lack of place, 117, 119
  meetings. *See* Meetings and
      ROWE
  payment based on results, 4, 71,
      105

  prioritizing, 131–32
  and productivity increase, 6, 101,
      120, 135, 153–54
  questioning value, 111–12, 225
  reaching others, methods of, 129,
      223–24
  results as focus of, 57–61, 70, 73
  skills versus job, 119–21
  slackers, lack of, 118, 223
  studio approach, 85
  teams. *See* Teams and ROWE
  time spent, control of. *See* Time
      and ROWE

CultureRx delivers the impact of ROWE: Results-Only Work Environment to organizations that want to harness this dramatic, global movement.

For more information about ROWE go to www.gorowe.com.

Visit www.caliandjody.com to find out more about the authors, to read their blog, and to book them to speak at your organization.

Penguin's Business-to-Business advantage program allows your local bookstore to offer special discounted pricing on this title for bulk sales. Your business or non-profit can receive special discounted pricing, great service, direct shipping, and more. Call your local bookstore and say you'd like to use Penguin's B2B program to buy copies of this book for giveaway or training.

———— *Why Work Sucks and How to Fix It* 978-1-59184-292-7 $15.00 ($18.50 CAN)